How To Build A Basic 3-String Cigar Box Guitar

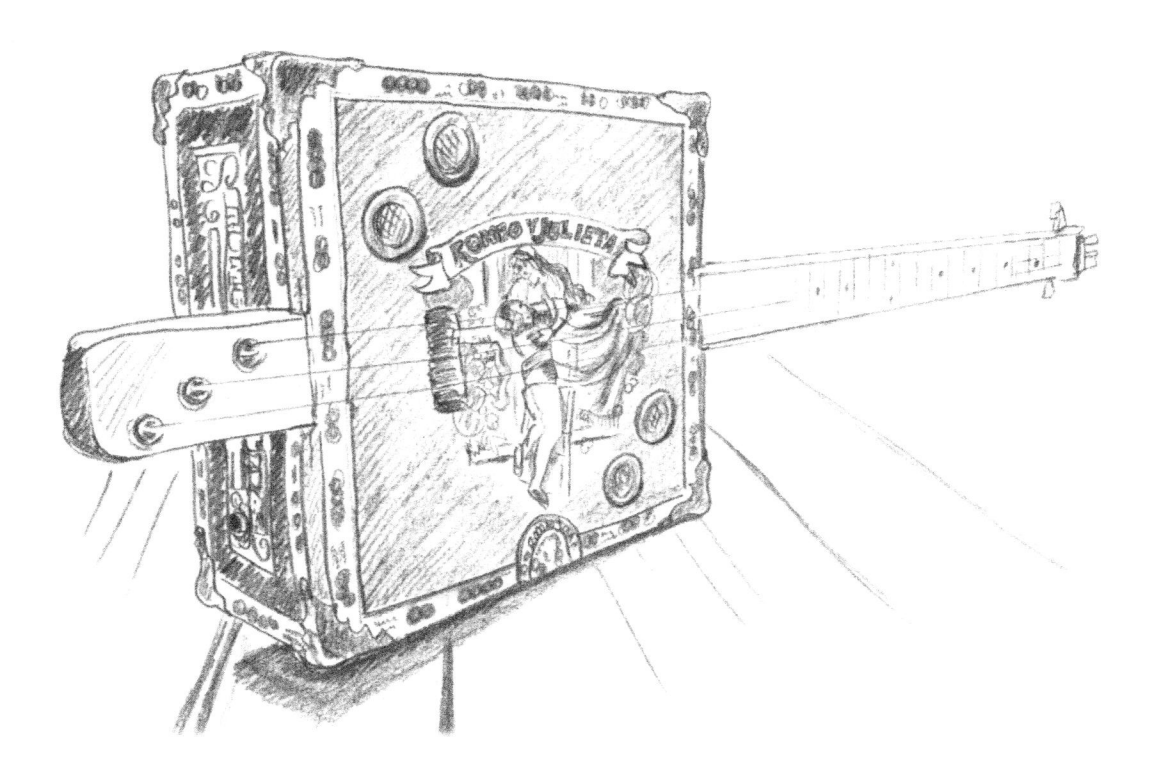

Ben "Gitty" Baker

A practical introduction to easily building your own fun and fully playable three-string cigar box guitar (CBG), complete with clear and detailed how-to instructions and photos, resource links, tips and tricks, how-to-play lessons, and more.

Copyright Notice

This original work is copyright 2019 by Hobo Music Works, LLC. Please do not reproduce this book, in whole or in part, without written permission from the author. Special permission for educational purposes may be available, please contact us at sales@hobofiddle.com to discuss options.

Table of Contents

Acknowledgements ... 4
Introduction ... 5
    Why Build a Cigar Box Guitar? ... 8
    Where Does Music Come From? ... 9
    A Trip Through Time ... 10
    People Find a Way ... 11
    Innovation Continues ... 16
    Make it Your Own ... 18
    Build What You Play, Play What You Love ... 20
    Welcome ... 22
Getting Ready ... 23
    Anatomy of a Cigar Box Guitar ... 23
    Safety Warning ... 26
    Let's Get Started ... 27
Sourcing Materials – An Illustrated Parts List ... 28
    The Cigar Box ... 28
        Cigar Box Size Recommendations ... 28
        Where to Find Cigar Boxes ... 30
    The Neck ... 34
    Strings ... 35
    Nut and Bridge ... 37
        Making a Wooden Nut (Optional) ... 38
    Tuners ... 39
    Tailpiece ... 42
    Decorative Embellishments (Optional) ... 44
        Sound Hole Treatments ... 44
        Box Corners ... 45
    Optional Hardware ... 47
        Strap Buttons ... 47
        Pickups ... 48

Table of Contents

    Pickguards — **49**
  Other Decorations and Embellishments — **50**

Tools — **55**
  Saw — **55**
  Drill — **56**
  Screwdriver — **57**
  Glue — **57**
  Wood File and Sandpaper — **57**
  Ruler — **58**
  Other Tools — **58**

Build Instructions — **60**
  1. Prepare Your Workspace and Tools — **60**
  2. Cut the Neck to Length — **61**
  3. Measure and Cut the Headstock Recess — **61**
  4. Sand and Smooth the Headstock Cutout — **62**
  5. Mark Center Points of Cigar Box and Neck — **64**
  6. Mark the Neck Notches on the Cigar Box End Panels — **66**
  7. Cut the Neck Notches into the Cigar Box — **67**
  8. Determining Neck Placement in the Box — **70**
  9. Mark the Neck for Box Recess Cut — **71**
  10. Cut the Neck Recess — **73**
  11. Prepping and Installing the Tailpiece — **77**
    Neck Heel String Anchoring — **77**
    Hinge Tailpiece Method — **78**
  12. Drill the Sound Holes — **81**
  13. Do Final Shaping/Sanding of Neck and Apply Finish (Optional) — **88**
  14. Install the Tuners/Machine Heads — **90**
    Determining Your Tuner Alignment — **92**
    Marking Tuner Hole Location — **92**
    Drill the Tuner Holes — **94**

How To Build A Basic 3-String Cigar Box Guitar · Copyright 2019 by Hobo Music Works LLC · All Rights Reserved

Table of Contents

Installing the Tuners	**96**
14. Install the Nut	**100**
15. Install Box Corners (Optional)	**102**
16. Seal the Box (Optional)	**103**
17. String It Up	**103**
Congratulations!	**108**
Tuning and Playing	**109**
Slide Playing	**109**
Fret Position Marking	**110**
Fret Position Table for 25-inch Scale Length	**111**
Playing Your First Song	**112**
Playing Your Second Song	**112**
Troubleshooting	**113**
Buzzing Strings	**113**
Broken Strings	**113**
Over Cuts, Mis-drilled Holes and Other Problems	**114**
Closing Thoughts	**115**
Appendix 1 - Measurement Conversions Chart	**117**
Appendix 2 - Common Scale Length Charts	**118**
References and Resources	**132**
Educational Outreach	**136**
Buyer's Guide	**137**

Acknowledgements

This book would never have been possible without the help, encouragement and advice of many people over the years.

I can't thank enough the amazing team of people who have joined me to make C. B. Gitty Crafter Supply what it is: Kim Starling, Glenn Watt, Laurel Caldwell, Jason Munoz, Dawn "Mrs. Gitty" Baker, Shereen Garland, Nick Lanciano, R. J. McCarty, Jake Letourneau, Danny Woodman and Cheryl Caldwell.

My wife Dawn Baker deserves extra thanks beyond her work at C. B. Gitty, for putting up with me and my shenanigans—musical and otherwise.

Mr. Shane Speal for being a great friend, mentor, motivator, instigator and creative partner in this endeavor.

All of the customers of C. B. Gitty Crafter Supply, whose trust and faith in us and our products helps keep the wheels turning and the mission moving forward. Thank you so much for your support over the years.

Members of Cigar Box Nation and the entire world-wide cigar box guitar and homemade music movement—thank you so much for sharing your photos, videos, stories, advice, questions and friendship over the years.

And finally a mention of the man in whose footsteps I follow, who did so much to help make me who I am today: my grandfather Irvin Baker Jr.

Grandpa Baker checking out a hand-made canjo.

Introduction

BUILDING A CIGAR BOX GUITAR IS EASY... ESPECIALLY ONCE YOU KNOW HOW!

Above: Ben "Gitty" Baker, author of this guide, holding one of his creations in the C. B. Gitty workshop in Rochester, New Hampshire. This particular cigar box guitar is a four-string build that features a stainless steel dog bowl as a resonator.

Thank you for purchasing this guide and deciding to try your hand at building your own cigar box guitar. On the pages that follow, I will be walking you through this fun and fulfilling process... but first, I'll be digging into the "why's and wherefores" behind all of it. We'll be looking at where these instruments come from, why creating a hand-crafted cigar box guitar is something worth doing, and what role cigar box guitars and other homemade instruments play in the modern music scene.

Before getting into all of that, you may be wondering who I am and what qualifies me to write a guide like this. Handmade instrument building isn't the sort of thing you go to school for – there are no degrees, certifications or letters to put after your name. Pretty much all of us are self-taught, figuring it out as we go.

I built my first CBG over a decade ago. My path to homemade instrument building started when some friends gave me a canjo as a gift, which they had picked up down in Gatlinburg, Tennessee. If you don't know, a canjo is a simple one-string instrument that uses a beer or soda can as a resonator... basically a can, a stick, and a string. (I've since built dozens of canjos and even written a book about how to build them, if you want to learn more: CBGitty.com/BuildACanjo).

Above: The canjo that started the author on his path to homemade instrument building.

I took that canjo and played a couple of tunes on it, and then said, "Well heck, I could build one of these!" I got online and started searching, and while I didn't find much about canjos, I did discover another handmade instrument: the cigar box guitar. Back in those days there were only a couple of mentions on websites, and Shane Speal's Yahoo discussion group with a couple of hundred dedicated members. I managed to find some free plans on how to build, and I was off.

Over time in my own building, and in talking with other members of the CBG community, it became clear that finding inexpensive guitar parts was harder than it should be. So even though I had no official business training, I began sourcing and reselling certain parts that CBG builders needed. I named my fledgling company C. B. Gitty Crafter Supply. The "C. B." stands for "Cigar Box" and "Gitty" is slang for guitar. Originally my goal was just to help fund my own building hobby, but over time it grew into something far beyond anything I had imagined.

Now, over ten years later, C. B. Gitty is the premiere world-wide supplier of instruments, kits, parts and gear for the homemade music movement. We stock over a thousand different parts (over four hundred of them manufactured in-house), and have created dozens of innovative kits, tools, templates and guides to help homemade instrument builders along.

We have also created an extensive free knowledgebase site (www.CigarBoxGuitar.com) chock full of free plans and information, including how-to-build and how-to-play articles and videos, as well as owning and operating www.CigarBoxNation.com. C. B. Gitty is proud to sponsor many cigar box guitar festivals around the United States, and helps support traveling home-made instrument musicians.

All of this experience with building homemade instruments, designing kits, sourcing and using parts, and interacting with other builders, goes into the creation of this guide. I will do my best to pour out everything I have learned about the specific subject of building a 3-string slide CBG, in the clearest and easiest to understand form possible.

Thank you again, and happy building!

Why Build A Cigar Box Guitar?

***Above:** Artist and cigar box guitar builder Farley Andresen holds an "Old Glory" cigar box guitar she built in the C. B. Gitty workshop.*

This is a question that a lot of folks who are new to the concept might ask themselves: why bother? In a world where there are so many inexpensive mass-produced "real" guitars out there, why would a person want to take the time to build a primitive, handmade, three-stringed instrument out of a second-hand cigar box?

To answer that, we must dig right down into what music really means. In today's world, it seems sometimes like the powers that be want us to think that "real" music, and musical instruments, only come down from one source: the corporate music industry. Whether it's the latest auto-tuned pop music production, or the shiny new factory-made name-brand acoustic hanging on the wall down at the big-box guitar store, it can feel like we just have to take what we're given and be happy with it.

We must ask ourselves… is that really what music is all about?

Where Does Music Come From?

For thousands of years, folks have been making their own music and musical instruments. What we have today is built upon these millennia of regular people experimenting, learning, crafting and creating.

Far back into our prehistoric past, music has resonated deep within the human psyche, and there have always been those who struggled to find their own way to bring forth into the world the songs they had in their soul. Over time professional instrument-makers emerged, but it began with amateurs.

There is something deep and meaningful in playing a musical instrument you've built yourself. It doesn't matter how primitive it might be. To have used your own hands and ingenuity to craft a piece of art (the instrument) which can in turn be used to create more art (music) is special on a primal level. Even if you're not a musician and have never plucked a note, hearing those first sounds ring out from your new creation is a magical moment.

The cigar box guitar you will build using this guide is a simple one – it could be described as just a stick, some strings, and a box… but it will be YOURS. It will be your unique, one-of-a-kind handmade creation, a musical instrument that harkens back across the eons and strikes at the very heart of our human need to bring music forth into the world.

Above: One possible example of a 3-string slide cigar box guitar that can be built using this guide. Depending on your choices of neck wood, cigar box style, sound holes and other factors, your build will look uniquely different from this one.

You may think I'm going a little overboard with this. It's just a stick stuffed through a cigar box, with some tightened guitar strings running over it, right? It's not gonna change the world, right?

Well, why not?

A Trip Through Time

Imagine back in the mists of history, one of our ancestors noticing that when he hit a hollow log with his club in just the right way, the sound that rang out was interesting. When he tapped another part, a subtly different sound came forth.

Imagine an ancient woman when she first noticed that when a wet animal skin was stretched over a pot, and lashed fast to keep the contents secure, that when the skin dried and became tight, it could be tapped with a spoon to make a pleasing sound.

Imagine the hunter who first discovered, while using his teeth to tighten the knot on the gut string of his hunting bow, that if he plucked the string while the end of the bow was in his mouth, the hum of the string would be amplified in interesting ways.

Above: A Nigerian man plays a mouth bow, which originated as a standard hunting bow and evolved into an instrument designed specifically for making music.

Think of the uncounted thousands of people over the years, from these humble beginnings, who took what was already known and tried something new, and who rejoiced in each discovery and the amazing new sounds they coaxed from their instruments. If they failed along the way, they learned from it and tried again.

Knowledge and methods were handed down over the generations, centuries and millennia. The hunting/mouth bow evolved into basic harps and lyres, and then to lutes and citterns, and then branched out into violins, cellos, mandolins and guitars. Percussion and wind instruments followed their own paths of expansion and evolution.

People Find a Way

In more recent times, poor folks have turned to handmade and homemade instruments when they couldn't afford "the real thing." Union soldiers in the American Civil War fashioned fiddles from cigar boxes, as documented in the engravings of Edwin Forbes shown below.

Above: The two best-known sketches by Edwin Forbes from the American Civil War, showing Union soldiers making and playing cigar box fiddles. The top image was inscribed "Making of Cremona", and the bottom one "Home Sweet Home". Forbes sketched these while traveling with the Union army, and they are believed to depict actual scenes he witnessed.

Street urchins in New Orleans in the late 1800's and early 1900's also made cigar box guitars, fiddles and washtub basses and performed wild "spasm band" music on street corners and in brothels around the Storyville district of the "Big Easy". Some believe that their music and that of other spasm bands, heard by adult musicians in the area, may have influenced the creation of Jazz music.

Above: An 1899 photo of the "Razzy Dazzy Spasm Band" in New Orleans, a band of street urchins who played homemade instruments. Their wild style of music is believed by some to have helped inspire the creation of Jazz music. The band was led by Emile "Stalebread Charlie" Lacoume, and had other members with names such as Harry Gregson, "Whiskey" Benrod, "Cajun" and "Monk" Bussey, "Chinee", "Family Haircut" and one boy known only as "Warm Gravy."

In the Mississippi delta region in the early 1900's, many poor folks built their own guitars out of cigar boxes and other materials... and some of them went on to become the founding fathers of the Blues. Lightnin' Hopkins, Mississippi John Hurt, Little Freddie King, Albert King, Muddy Waters... so many of the greats got their start with a humble cigar box guitar.

Above: Artist Farley Andresen's interpretation of an old blues man playing music on his homemade cigar box guitar in the Mississippi delta region in the 1920's. Cigar box guitars, diddley bows and other homemade instruments played an important role in the development of the musical genre we now know as the Blues. Many of the musicians that we now consider as founders of the Blues got their start on handmade instruments that they built themselves.

In the Appalachian region, enterprising homesteaders often crafted their own banjos, fiddles, dulcimers and other instruments. The Foxfire series of books catalogs some of their building methods, and are a recommended resource.

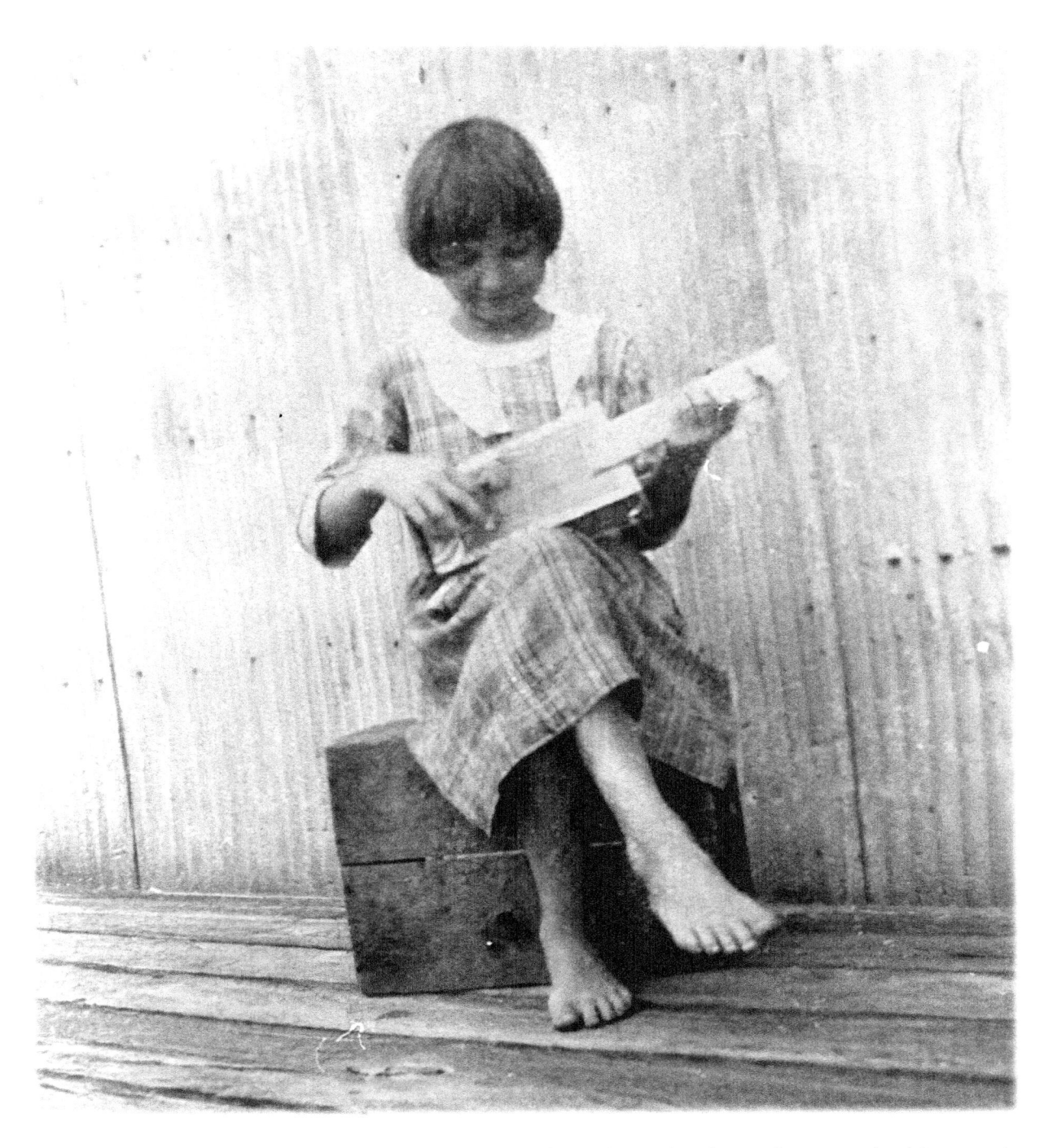

Above: Photo of unknown date and origin, but thought to be from the Appalachian region of the United States, of a young girl playing a homemade cigar box instrument. There is a long tradition of hand-crafting fiddles, banjos, dulcimers and other instruments throughout the Appalachian Mountains.

In Africa, South America and other less-developed areas of the world, people are still crafting musical instruments from gas cans, steel drums and other scavenged items. For them, it isn't just a fun hobby... often it's they only way they have of making music. People always find a way – when the music is in them, they create what they need to let it out.

Above: A child in Africa plays a simple homemade guitar he built from scavenged materials. Whereas many of us choose to build our own instruments even though we can afford store-bought ones, in less developed areas of the world people have no choice but to build their own. Malawi and Liberia are two areas in Africa known for homemade musical instruments.

INNOVATION CONTINUES

It can be tempting to slip into the mindset that everything has already been done, that there is "nothing new under the sun," and that new development of musical instruments ended long ago... but that is not the case. Or you may think that any new work being done today must be in the realm of electronic music, using computers and synthesizers to produce the sounds – and while much is being done in that field, it is not the only area of innovation.

There is a thriving culture of DIY musical instrument builders all around the world, crafting and creating in their basements, garages, sheds and even at their kitchen tables. The vast majority of us are not trained luthiers, and most of us never took a class in how this sort of thing is supposed to be done.

We are not afraid to try new things to see if they work; and when they don't, we learn from the failure and move on. In many ways, not being bound by the conventional way of doing things frees us to be more experimental and inventive in our own building. Sometimes, not knowing what you "shouldn't" do frees you up to try things a professional never would, with surprising results.

Making musical instruments out of reclaimed, everyday items that were never meant to have a voice, requires constant innovation, creative problem solving and DIY ingenuity.

A hand-sketched rendition of a detail from the Cigar Box Nation logo. For over a decade, CigarBoxNation.com has been the nerve center of the worldwide cigar box guitar movement. It remains the largest online community of DIY instrument builders, with over 20,000 members and counting. You can join the site for free and become a part of the thriving group of homemade music enthusiasts.

Make it Your Own

Building guitars, ukuleles and other instruments from reclaimed materials such as cigar boxes, which were never intended to make music or have a voice, is uniquely rewarding. Once you start, it can be hard to stop. You begin looking at the world in a new way, thinking about how everyday objects could be turned into musical instruments.

Whether walking through a big box hardware store, visiting an antique or junk store, going through the attic, or stopping at a yard sale or flea market, you may find yourself somewhat obsessed, with the mantra "I could make a guitar out of that!" running through your mind.

Above: A workbench full of items collected with (mostly) instrument-building in mind! You may find (as the author did) that it's a lot easier to collect neat stuff for potential instruments, than it is to actually make the instruments!

Spouses, friends and neighbors may not understand, and that's OK. Professional musicians and the folks at your local guitar store may not "get it," and may even scoff at your creations. Don't worry about that – these instruments are not for purists and the closed-minded. People may call your creations toys, and say they don't compare to "real" guitars. Don't let that bother you.

I don't call store-bought guitars "real" anymore... I call them "conventional". To me, a cigar box guitar I built myself is about as REAL as it gets. It is true that my cigar box guitar will never make the sounds that a Martin D-28 can... but then again, a Martin D-28 will never make the sounds that my cigar box guitar can. I have come to love that difference. Make the music that is meaningful to you – even if others don't understand it.

If you have children in your life, they'll probably instinctively get it, and maybe even want to help you build. Do your best to encourage them! Kids especially appreciate the connection to something they created (and ideally decorated) themselves. Hand a kid a store-bought guitar and tell them to learn to play it, and there's a pretty good chance it won't take. Help them build their own handmade guitar, however, and you've planted a seed that has a much higher chance of taking root.

Above: If you have kids in your life, involve them in your instrument building! They especially love helping to decorate cigar boxes.

BUILD WHAT YOU PLAY, PLAY WHAT YOU LOVE

Cigar box guitars and related homemade instruments are about getting back to the roots of music, down to the fundamentals of what it means and why it's important. You don't need a shiny, mass-produced, store-bought guitar to make music. All you need is a stick, a box, some strings and a little bit of hardware, and you'll be on your way. Build what you play, and play what you love… and remember that if you're having fun, you're doing it right.

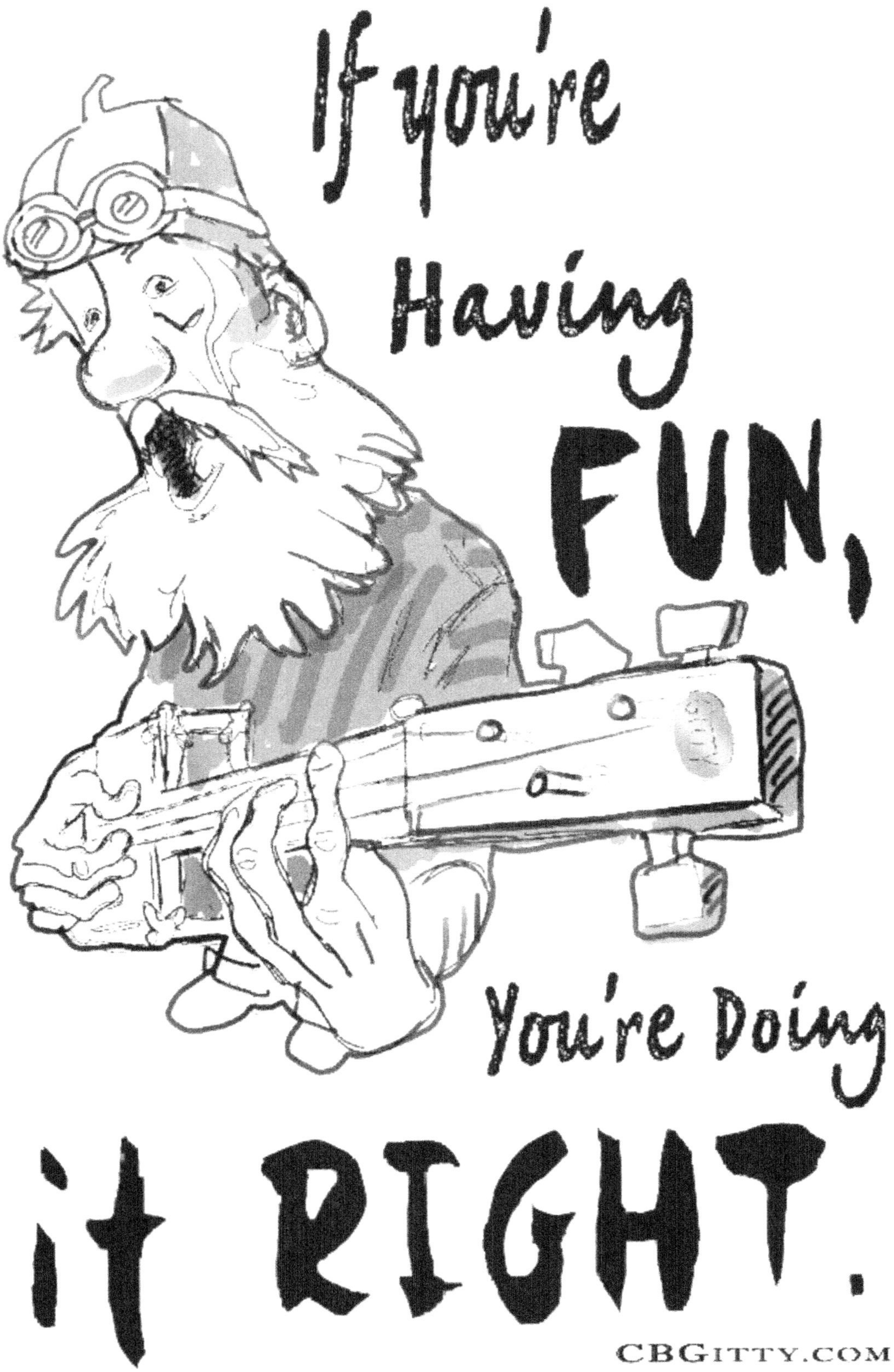
If you're
Having
FUN,
You're Doing
it RIGHT.
CBGITTY.COM

Welcome

By purchasing this guide and deciding to build your own cigar box guitar, you are joining the global community of homemade and handmade instrument-builders. You are helping to spread the word that ANYONE, ANYWHERE can build their own guitar and make music on it. I have made it my life's mission to spread this message, and my company C. B. Gitty Crafter Supply furthers that cause by providing parts, kits, gear and how-to materials to people all around the world.

I hope that you enjoy this journey through crafting your own cigar box guitar, that making music on it brings you joy, and that you'll catch a little bit of the "building bug" and want to build more. I believe that all of us, together, making our own music like this helps make the world just a little bit better.

Getting Ready

This section will walk you through all of the preliminaries that need to be sorted out before you can get busy building. First we'll go over the key parts of a cigar box guitar, then cover some safety guidelines.

We'll then move on to tips for finding the parts and materials you'll need for your cigar box guitar, and finally talk about the necessary tools and workspace requirements.

ANATOMY OF A CIGAR BOX GUITAR

Before we dive into sourcing parts and building, it will help things along if we identify some of the key parts on a CBG so we're on the same page going forward.

The image below shows all the parts of a "Cadillac" model box guitar, much fancier than the one we'll be building in this guide. Though many of the items shown in this image won't come into play on what you'll be building, having an idea of what they are will help you through the process.

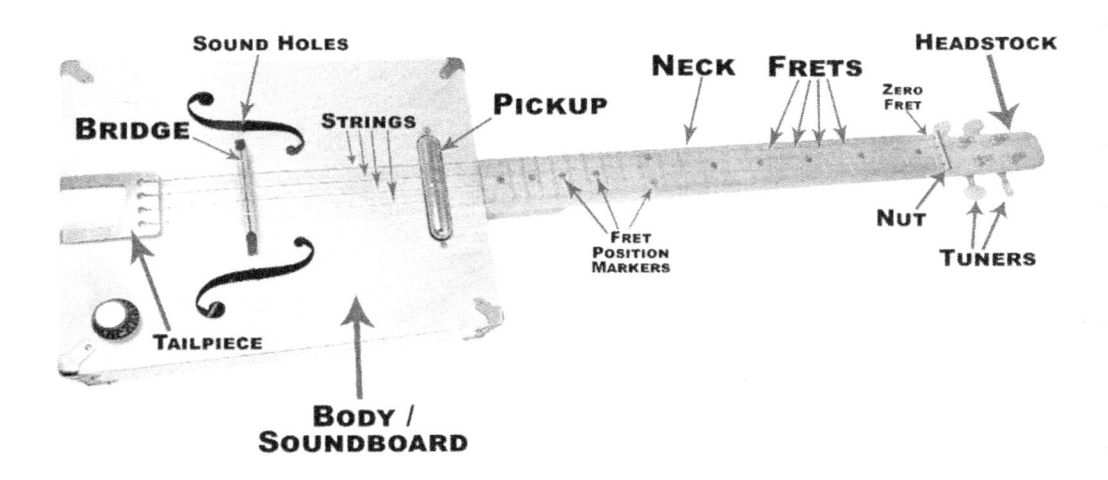

Above: A 4-string box guitar, assembled from a C. B. Gitty "Tupelo Tenor" DIY kit, labeled to identify key parts. Many of the items shown here

are more advanced and optional, and will not be used on the cigar box guitar we'll be building in this guide. The box corners and volume control knob are not labeled.

Another key concept to understand is "Scale Length", which directly affects the overall size of the instrument and how it plays. The diagram below shows that scale length is simply the distance between the NUT at the top of the neck and the BRIDGE on the instrument body. The strings run from the tuner posts in the headstock, up and over the nut, then down the neck and over the body, over the bridge, and are fastened to the butt end of the instrument, whether via a tailpiece or anchored directly into the neck.

Another way of putting it is that the scale length is the total vibrating length of the strings: the measurement between where the strings leave the nut and where they first touch the bridge.

The cigar box guitar we'll be building in this guide will have a scale length of 25 inches (635mm).

Scale Length
Distance from Nut to Bridge

Above: This diagram illustrates the definition of "scale length" in relation to a cigar box guitar.

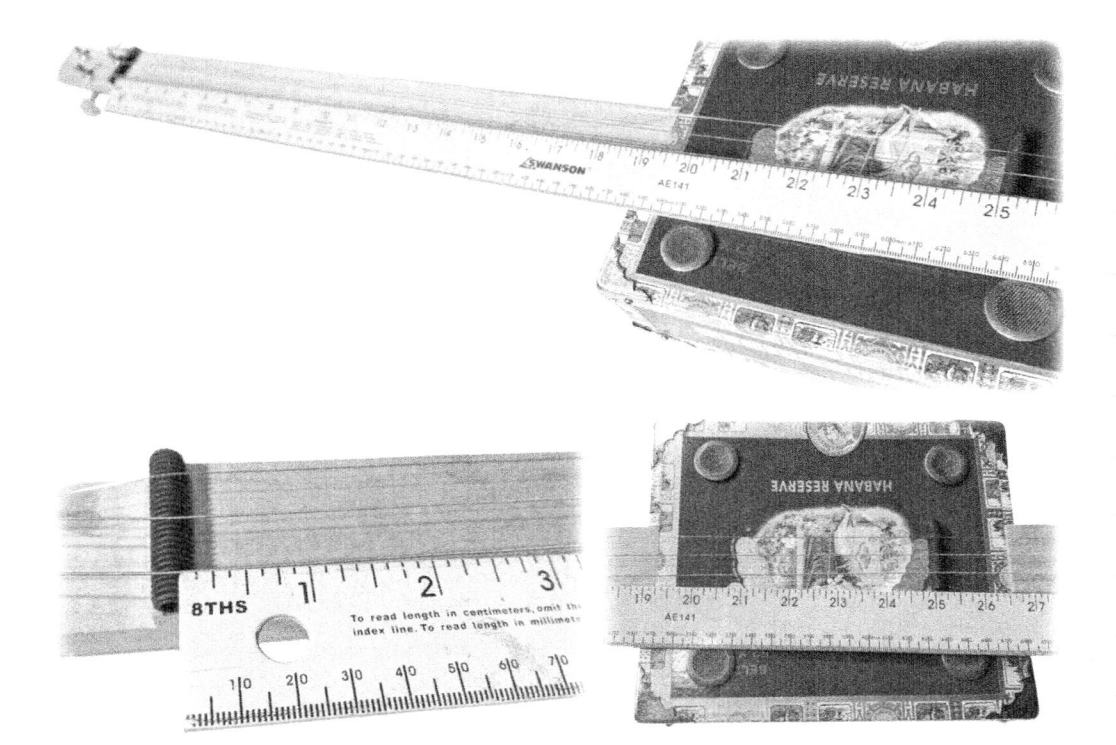

Above: These photos demonstrate the measurement of scale length on an actual cigar box guitar, which happens to be the one built in the photographs throughout this guide.

Safety Warning

Before grabbing any tools, please give some serious thought to your own safety, and that of anyone who may be working with you – especially any younger children.

The steps described in this guide will require the use of basic woodworking tools, whether hand tools or powered. You will be cutting wood with a saw, drilling holes, sanding and filing and inserting screws. Please follow all manufacturer warnings and usage guidelines for the tools you will be using.

Wood dust and other small particles will be generated during the cutting and sanding operations described in this guide. Be sure to wear a dust mask and ensure proper ventilation in your work area. Also be careful of splinters and sharp edges on wooden pieces.

Wear eye protection during any cutting, drilling, sanding or other operation that can potentially create eye-damaging situations.

There will also be some small parts, such as screws, that could be a choking hazard to children.

Let's Get Started

OK, enough philosophy and sermonizing... what you really want is to get busy building your cigar box guitar, right? I don't blame you. We are going to work our way through the process one step at a time, from sourcing the materials you'll need, to preparing your tools and workspace, to the actual construction, to getting her strung and tuned. At the very end, we'll even walk through playing your first couple of songs!

This guide takes you through building a three-string slide (unfretted) cigar box guitar (CBG). Because there are many ways to build such an instrument, and many varieties of parts and hardware that can used, what I am going to do is present a fairly basic and straightforward method using commonly available tools and parts.

When appropriate I may mention alternate methods and hardware, but my goal is to keep this guide as focused as possible. If you are interested in more advanced methods, be sure to check the resources list at the end of this guide for ideas!

I recommend reading all the way through the instructions before starting any building – it can be very helpful to already have an idea of where you are going to end up, before you start.

Above: The contents of one of C. B. Gitty's most popular basic cigar box guitar kits. Some of the items (box corners and sound hole inserts) are optional decorative elements that can be added if desired.

Sourcing Materials — An Illustrated Parts List

As you begin gathering the parts you'll use to build your CBG, please keep in mind that none of it has to be perfect. Cigar box guitars are meant to be somewhat primitive, to have some rough edges, to have a bit of buzz and twang, and other unique personality traits. It isn't meant to be a shiny, polished and perfect thing. Those idiosyncrasies will give your instrument its unique character.

So, try to stay relaxed and not stress too much about everything being just right. Always remember that no matter how badly you think you are messing up, it will still probably be alright... and you'll learn a lot of great lessons for when you build your next one!

The Cigar Box

The cigar box is the heart of the cigar box guitar, forming the body of the instrument. Its lid has the biggest impact on the overall tone of the instrument. In general, thinner lids are better than thicker (but not so thin that it can't stand up to the downward pressure of the bridge), and plywood is somewhat better than MDF/hardboard (though MDF will still work just fine). Try to avoid boxes made from softer cardboard.

Cigar Box Size Recommendations

In general, you want to find a wider, flatter cigar box, as opposed to one of the more cube-like boxy ones. There is no hard rule on minimum size, but in general you'll be in good shape if you can find one at least **7.5 inches wide (~190mm), 5.5 inches tall (140mm) and 1.25 inches (32mm) deep**.

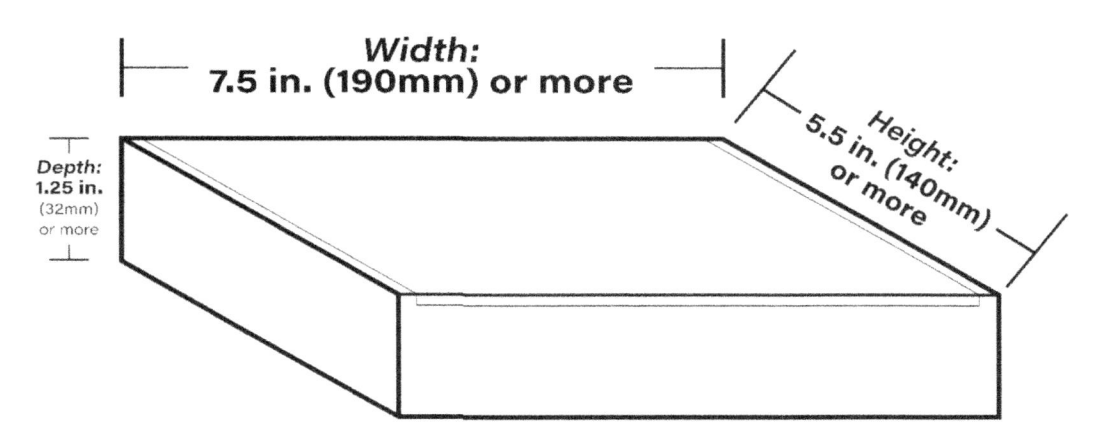

Above: This diagram shows the wider and flatter style of cigar box recommended for use in building cigar box guitars, and gives the minimum size recommendations for each dimension.

An all-(ply)wood box is great if you can find one, but paper covered MDF/hardboard varieties will do just fine (and are generally easier to find).

Try to find a cigar box where the lid closes into the body, as is shown in the first sample image below. Note that its general shape is a wider, flatter rectangle. Also notice how the lid seats down flush into the body of the box.

Above: An example of a perfect size and style of cigar box for building the CBG detailed in this guide.

You may only be able to find a box like the one shown below, which has a different "clamshell" style of lid arrangement. Note how the join between the lid and the body is further down, and that there are side-wall portions to the lid. You can certainly use a box of this style... you will just have to handle it a little differently later when we are cutting notches for the neck. Basically, instead of cutting a single notch opening into the end walls of main body of the box, you will divide the notch between the body and the lid portions.

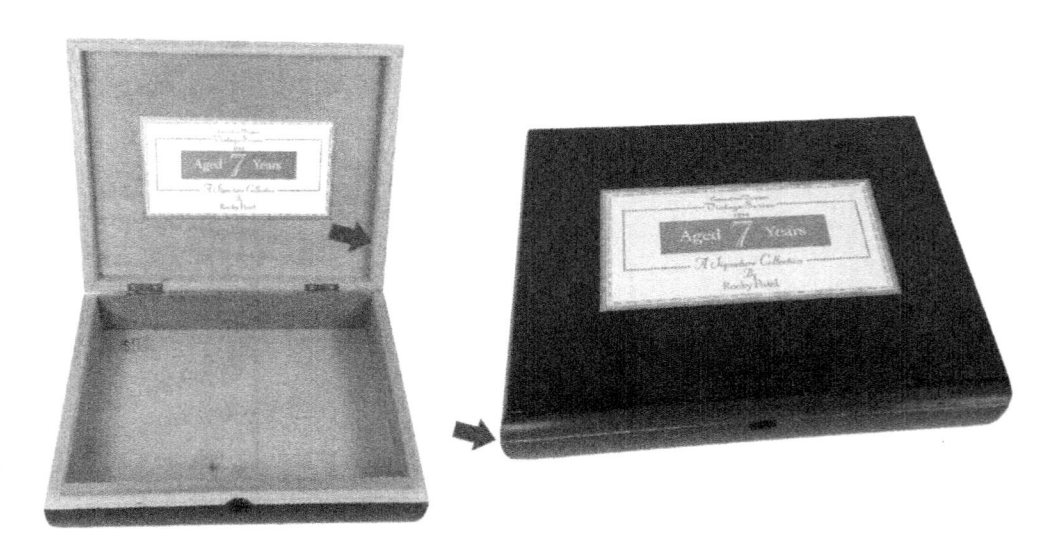

Above: An all-wood cigar box with a clamshell style lid. While this style of box can work great for cigar box guitars, using one does require slight changes to the neck notching and mounting methods described later in this guide.

Where to Find Cigar Boxes

To find cigar boxes in the United States, you have a few options. Check around for a local cigar shop, or any convenience/smoke/vape store that also sells cigars. Usually they will have a few empties that you can either have for free, or pick up for a couple of dollars.

You can also check around at garage sales, flea markets and similar events, often there will be a few old cigar boxes to be found – especially at indoor flea markets that tend to set up at the same place on weekends all year round. You can often find vintage boxes at such events, sometimes for pretty cheap. If you are able to find an old all-wood box of the Corina Larks brand or similar, with solid cedar panels, that makes for a great-sounding cigar box guitar… though you might want to practice your first build with a less desirable box.

Above: The top photo shows a collection of modern cigar boxes, some of which are well-suited for use in cigar box guitar building. The bottom photo shows a collection of vintage all-wood "Corina" brand cigar boxes, with solid cedar panels. These vintage all-wood boxes tend to have very good tone and with careful use are great for cigar box guitar building.

If you just can't find any local source of boxes, you can always go online. There are many options to be found on eBay, though the price with shipping can sometimes be a bit more than you'd want to pay – especially if they have to be shipped internationally. Other online sellers, such as CBGitty.com, also sells a range of cigar boxes suited for homemade instrument building.

Above: A three-string guitar built by the author from an old wooden explosives crate. The original crate was too large and "boxy" for a guitar body, so he took it apart, resized some of the panels, and built the wider, flatter box seen above.

For would-be cigar box guitar builders in countries other than the United States, finding a cigar box can be much harder, especially in Europe and Australia.

In these countries cigar-smoking is not as common, and often shops will return empty boxes to the manufacturers. Those boxes that do become available are often plastered with large anti-smoking messages that include gruesome images of diseased lungs or teeth – definitely not great for instrument-building.

Our international friends can certainly cough up the cash to have a box shipped from the U. S., but **here's a dirty little secret about cigar box guitars: you don't actually have to use a cigar box to build one**. You can use a wooden silverware box, jewelry box, wine box, fruit crate or other such thing as the body.

You can even make your own box out of thin wood pieces if you must. Some builders even make guitars out of biscuit and cookie tins. The building process changes a bit, but the spirit of the result is the same. The point is, you use what is available to you and make it work.

Above: Savvy builders know that you don't need an actual cigar box to build a cigar box guitar. Though some purists argue about whether it is truly a CBG without the "CB", I've never let it bother me. A guitar handmade from reclaimed materials is a wonderful thing, whether or not it started from a cigar box. The photo above shows the results of a crate-buying expedition by the author. None of these wooden crates (except for the wooden cigar box top right) are well-suited to be turned into a

guitar as-is, but they can be taken apart, the panels trimmed down (with a focus on the ones that have stenciling/lettering), and rebuilt into an appropriately sized box. The moral of the story is this: don't let a lack of cigar boxes stop you from building!

The Neck

***Above:** A typical 1 x 2" piece of red oak dimensional lumber, perfect for use as a cigar box guitar neck.*

Basically, the neck of a cigar box guitar is a wooden stick, milled to dimensions within a certain range, which gets mounted into the cigar box to support the strings.

For the CBG we'll be building in this book, I recommend finding a standard "one by two" hardwood board 34 inches long. Often dimensional lumber of this sort can be found at big-box hardware stores such as Lowes, Home Depot, Menards and others. 1 in. x 2 in. is the "nominal" size of the board – in reality, it measures 0.75 inch by 1.5 inches (~19mm x ~38mm). In other countries, the exact dimensions might vary a little from this, but that's OK.

Here is a rough range of neck board sizes that should work just fine for building the cigar box guitar in this guide:

Width: Between 1.25 and 2 inches (~32mm to ~50mm) – 1.5 inches (~38mm) recommended

Thickness: 0.75 to 1 inch (~19mm to 25.4mm) – 0.75 inch recommended.

Length: 32 to 36 inches (~812mm to ~914mm) – 34 inches recommended

I strongly recommend using some type of hardwood (oak, maple, walnut, or even poplar) for your neck, as opposed to a softwood like pine or fir. Hardwood is much better at handling the tension of the strings without bowing. Because this cigar box guitar will be played with a slide, a bit of neck bowing isn't a big issue, but if at all possible, try to find a hardwood stick. If you just can't find one, go ahead and proceed with the sturdiest piece of softwood you can find.

Try to find a stick that is fairly smooth, without any large cracks, knots or splinters. You can always sand out smaller rough areas, but any major defects will be a problem later. You don't want anything that will make the cigar box guitar uncomfortable to hold and play, and you also don't want anything that will weaken the neck, like big knots or cracks.

You can of course mill down your own neck from a larger board if you wish and have the tools to do it. Often builders will use reclaimed wood of some sort for this, and if you can use a piece of wood that has some historic or personal meaning, all the better.

STRINGS

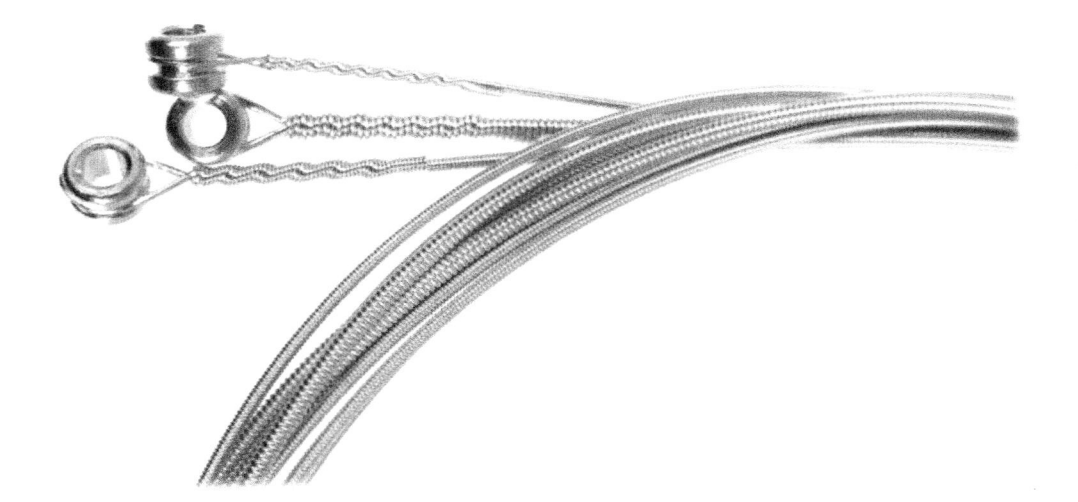

Above: A set of three "Blues Blaster" strings for Open G GDG tuning.

NOTES

The strings you choose for your cigar box guitar will determine its tuning, tone and how it is played. There are many different tunings that folks use for their CBGs, but by far the most common is one known as "Open G - GDG". This means that the three strings, from lowest to highest pitch, are tuned to G, D and another G – the second higher G being one octave in pitch above the lower one. Don't worry too much about that now, I'll discuss it in more detail when we cover stringing and tuning.

There are different ways to find the strings you'll need for Open G GDG tuning. One way is to take strings #5, #4 and #3 from a standard "Acoustic Medium" or "Acoustic Light" 6-string guitar pack. For those of you who know a little about 6-string guitars, that would be the A, D and G strings. Once on your cigar box guitar, that low A can be tuned down to a G, and voila, you have your G D G tuning.

Another option is to buy a set of strings specifically created for 3-string cigar box guitars tuned to Open G GDG. It so happens that at CBGitty.com/OpenG we have exactly what you need, all ready to go. If you go that route, choose either the "BLUES" option for a lower more growling blues tone, or the "FOLK/COUNTRY" option for a higher, twangier (more banjo-like) string set.

Here is a guide to string gauges to use for Low G and High G tunings with a 25-inch scale instrument such as the one you'll be building using this guide. It is generally better to stay on the lighter side when it comes to cigar box guitar strings, to keep the tension on the neck lower.

LOW G Tuning

- Low G: .042 to .044-inch bronze or nickel-wound
- Middle D: .030 to .034-inch bronze or nickel-wound
- High G: .022 to .026-inch bronze or nickel-wound

High G Tuning

- Low G: .022 to .026-inch bronze or nickel-wound

- Middle D: .012 to .014-inch plain steel
- High G: .009 to .010-inch plain steel

Nut and Bridge

As shown and described in the "Anatomy of a Cigar Box Guitar" images above, the nut and bridge are the two raised points on the guitar that the strings go up and over. The Nut is placed at the top of the neck/bottom of the headstock, and the bridge rests on the lid of the cigar box, which is also referred to as the "body" of the instrument, with its top (the box lid) being the "sound board".

BRIDGE   **NUT**

Above: Examples of threaded rod nut and bridge in use on a 3-string cigar box guitar.

A number of things can be used for the nut and bridge of a cigar box guitar. The photos above show a threaded rod being used for both, which is what we have been using in our basic cigar box guitar kits at C. B. Gitty for nearly a decade. Threaded rods work well because the threads automatically hold the strings in position without having to file grooves, and being round they come to a fine point at the top, which helps prevent string buzz (see below).

Some builders will use an eyebolt for the bridge and a hex bolt for the nut, allowing the head of the hex bolt to sit over the edge of the neck so it lays flat.

Other builders make their own nuts and bridges from wood, plastic, Corian, metal bar or rod stock, and even bone and antler. Basically, any hard, durable material that can be shaped to provide a narrow surface for the strings to go up and over can be used.

Here are some basic guidelines for making your own nut and bridge, though I recommend waiting until you have your headstock notched and the neck mounted in the box before crafting them, so you can adjust the measurements as needed.

Making a Wooden Nut (Optional)

Use hardwood if at all possible for your nut. Ideally you want the nut to be the same width as your neck, about 0.15 inches (3.8mm) thick, and tall enough to extend from the surface of your headstock up to above the surface of the neck by about 1/8 inch (0.125 in. / ~3.2mm). Based then on how deep you'll be recessing your headstock later in this guide, the rough size of your nut should be 1.5 inches (38.1mm) wide, 3/8 inch (0.375 / 9.5mm) tall and 0.15 inch (3.8mm) thick.

Sand or file a bevel onto what will be the top edge of the nut, so that it ends up about 1/16 inch (0.625 in. / 1.6mm) wide across the width of its surface. You don't want the string sitting on a wider flat surface across the nut (or bridge), as that can cause the string to buzz when plucked.

The photos below show several handmade nut examples from wood and bone. Notice how each is flush with the edges of the neck, is mounted right up tight against the headstock edge of the fingerboard, and how a bevel has been filed into to decrease the width of the top edge.

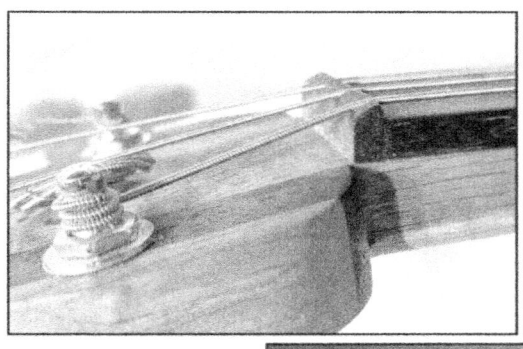

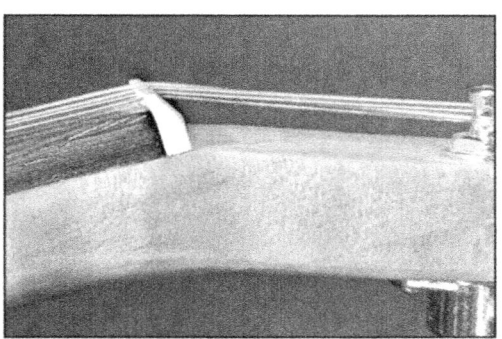

Above: Three different handmade nuts. Top left is made from padauk, top right from bone, and bottom center from black walnut. Note the bevel to narrow the top edge where the strings cross.

The photos above show the wooden nuts glued in place against a fretboard, with angled headstocks, which the cigar box guitar you'll be building with this guide won't have. Your nut will either rest on top of the neck itself (threaded rod), or be glued up against the notch of the recessed headstock – all of this will be clearly described once we get to the how-to steps.

PRO TIP: You may want to wait until you've read all the way through the how-to section before making a final decision on what type of nut to use.

Tuners

Tuners, also known as tuning pegs and machine heads, are the ingenious little devices that allow the tension (and thereby the tuning) of the strings to be easily changed.

NOTES

Above: A set of the classic C. B. Gitty Chrome Open-Gear Tuners, used by thousands of homemade instrument builders around the world on their cigar box guitars and other creations.

There have been many varieties of tuners over the years, from carved wooden pegs (still used on violins and related instruments) to finely threaded metal rods (called zither pins) that you need a special wrench to turn, to the specially geared modern machine heads used on most guitars today. Some homemade instrument builders go even further afield, using eyebolts and butterfly nuts or other such contraptions as makeshift tuners.

Above: The photos above show an example of handmade wooden tuner pegs, as crafted by master cigar box guitar builder Marty Tauber for his re-creation of an "Uncle Enos Banjo" from historic plans first published in the early 1880's.

You are certainly free to try carving your own violin-style tapered wooden pegs, or explore other tuner options if you want to for your first cigar box guitar. However, in this guide I'll be showing how to install and use standard open-gear modern machine heads.

These are the same ones we include in our various cigar box guitar and other DIY instrument kits here at C. B. Gitty, and thousands of first-time (and 100th-time) builders all around the world continue to have great success with them. You can pick up an inexpensive set from CBGitty.com/EconoTuners, or check your local guitar shops or other online sources for similar styles.

Above: Front and rear views of Chrome Economy Tuners installed on 3-string cigar box guitar headstocks.

Another option is to scavenge some tuners from an unwanted or broken guitar — you may already have one, or you can sometimes pick them up cheap at yard sales or flea markets. Instead of buying new, you can also check at your local guitar or music shop — ask them if they have an odds-and-ends box of guitar parts, explaining that you need three tuners for a special project. Often guitar shops will have all sorts of leftovers and spare parts that they will let go cheap, or even give away.

If you go this route, try hard to get three tuners that are all identical in style and design, and if at all possible get ones configured as shown in the photo above: with gears oriented towards the body, two tuners meant for mounting on the left side of the headstock (when viewed from the back), and one for mounting on the right. Finding tuners that match this configuration will make easier when we get to the tuner-mounting portion of the how-to steps.

Tailpiece

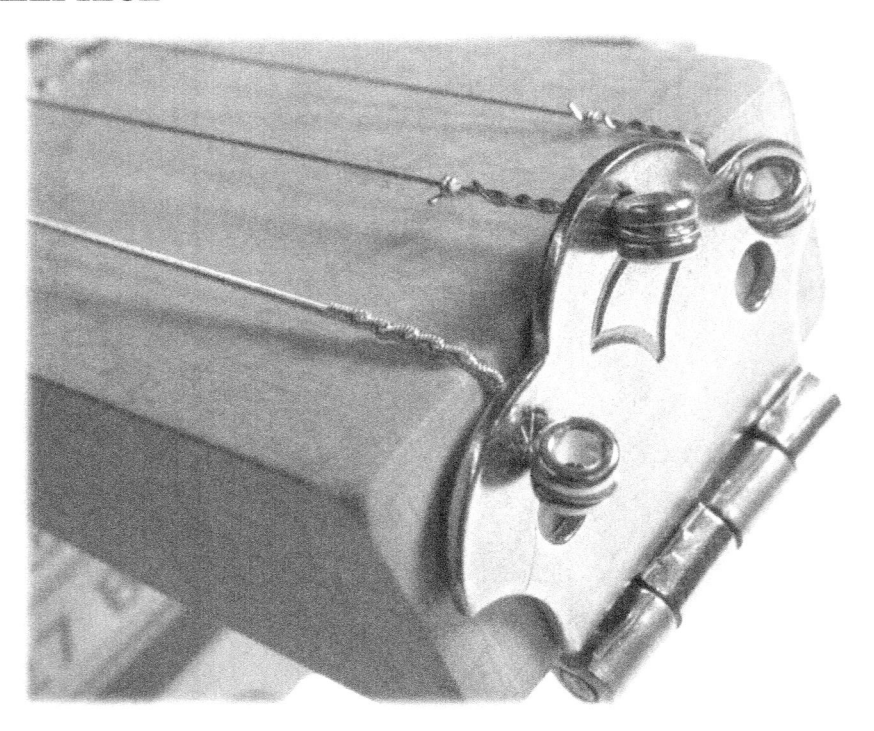

Above: A brass hinge used as a 3-string cigar box guitar tailpiece.

The tailpiece on a cigar box guitar serves to anchor the strings to the bottom end of the instrument. There are many different items that can be used to do this: specially made store-bought guitar tailpieces, metal hinges, hand-cut sheet metal creations, custom bent forks and spoons and much more.

With a neck-through style CBG such as the one we'll be building in this guide, there is another option that removes the need for a separate tailpiece altogether: string holes can be drilled through the butt end of the neck, and the strings fed up through them.

In this guide, we'll be showing both how to use a basic metal hinge as your cigar box guitar's tailpiece, as shown in the photo above, as well as how to drill string anchor holes in the neck heel. You can skip ahead to that section of the how-to steps to help you decide which method you want to use.

If you choose to employ a metal hinge as we did in the photo above, you may want to use a small-diameter drill bit to add three smaller holes hinge, instead of using the original larger holes that it originally came with. The photo below shows another example.

***Above:** An example of a hinge tailpiece mounted on the style of cigar box guitar you'll be building using this guide.*

Various types of smaller hinges will work for this, and you should be able to find something workable at your local hardware or big-box store. By smaller hinge, I mean something that is not much wider than your neck, and which will be able to be mounted to it as shown above without being too awkward.

If you want to browse some tailpieces made especially for cigar box guitars (including a pre-drilled version of the hinge shown in the photos above), check out CBGitty.com/tailpieces.

Decorative Embellishments (Optional)

There are many ways to "dress up" your cigar box guitar to help make it even more special and unique. The main ways builders do this is by some combination of decorating the cigar box, adding sound hole inserts/covers, adding box corners, and adding other decorative items/hardware.

Keep in mind that all of this is optional… you can just drill bare holes into your box for sound holes (or skip sound holes altogether if you want), leave the corners as they came, and call it done. It's all up to you – there are no rules about how YOUR cigar box guitar should look!

Sound Hole Treatments

If you look at the photo above, you will see small screened grommets have been glued into the sound holes on the face of the instrument. The sound holes themselves were drilled using a ½-inch (12.7mm) drill bit, and then the grommets were glued into place using a hot glue gun.

Smaller grommets (usually un-screened) can usually be found in small packs at hardware stores, and they work great for this purpose. The screened grommets seen in the photo are the style that we include with our basic 3-string CBG kits, and they are very popular.

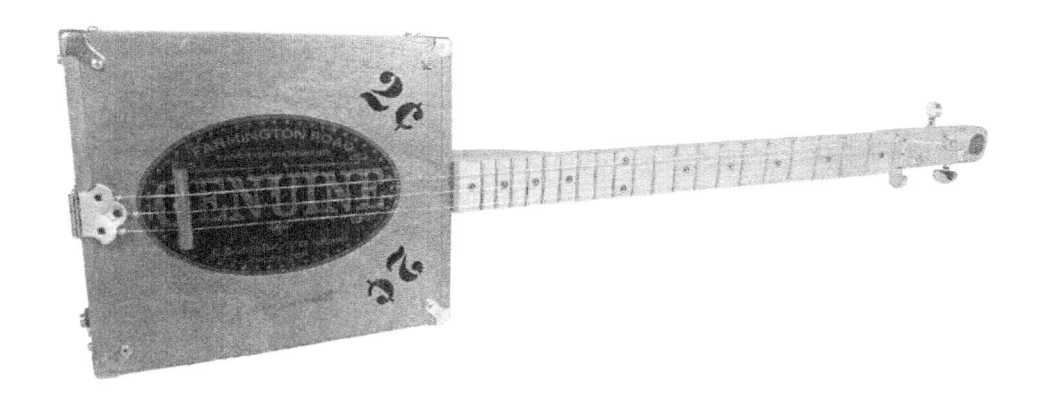

Above: a "2-cent Genny" 3-string cigar box guitar built in the C. B. Gitty shop, featuring special laser-cut "2¢" sound holes.

Another method is to drill a single larger hole and glue a bigger-diameter grommet into it. Some builders will use perforated sink drain inserts (found in the bathroom faucet repair aisle at hardware stores) as a sound hole insert. Others will drill/cut a nice clean hole, sand the edges, and put a layer or two of window screen under it, gluing/attaching the screen to the inside surface of the cigar box lid.

You can also make your own sound hole cover out of thin wood or plywood... or even using the thin veneer-type sheets of cedar that come in some cigar boxes. Shapes and styles are up to you.

Not to sound like a broken record, but maybe just one more time: remember that all of this is 100% optional and entirely decorative. Your sound hole(s) don't NEED to have anything glued into or covering them. So, if you just want to have plain drilled or sawed holes, then that's just fine.

You can even carve your own custom sound holes using a scroll saw, Dremel™ or other such tool.

Box Corners

Box and trunk corners are just metal pieces specially formed to fit over the corner point on wooden boxes (and other wooden items) to add a protective and decorative element. The past few photos in this guide have shown box corners installed on the instruments. While some prefer the look of the plain, unornamented cigar box corner, here at C. B. Gitty we usually put metal corners on most finished guitars. I just think it has a nice look, but it also serves to strengthen and protect those wooden (or MDF) box corners.

In many cases, corner pieces can also help hold the box lid closed, so that you don't have to mess around with screwing, nailing or gluing it shut! The photo below shows another angle of the "2-cent Genny" guitar pictured above, to more clearly show the brass corners. On these guitars, the corners were used to seal the box shut, so that if need be it could be re-opened later if the corners were removed.

Above: A close-up shot of a 3-string cigar box guitar with mini "trunk-style" brass-plated box corners installed. The corners serve three roles: decorative embellishment, protection of the wooden corner points, and sealing the cigar box lid closed.

When choosing box corners, there are a few things to watch out for. Think about where the screw holes will end up when placed on your cigar box. If one of the holes ends up over a lid closure seam, it may be tricky to get them securely mounted. If you choose trunk-style corners with longer arms (like those shown in the 2-cent Genny photos above), make sure your box is thick enough to have them mounted without overlap. Also, when planning your sound hole layout, make sure that your intended box corners won't end up overlapping the cutouts.

Optional Hardware

There are several optional hardware items you can add to your cigar box guitar, to make it more playable and versatile.

Strap Buttons

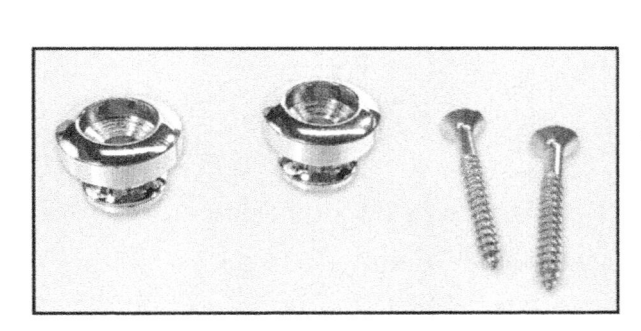

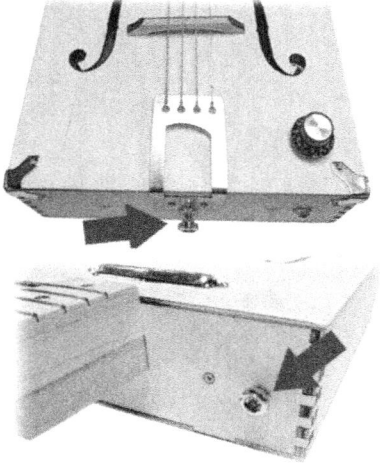

Above: Standard chrome guitar strap buttons, and an installation example on C. B. Gitty's "Tupelo Tenor" four-string DIY box guitar kit.

Strap buttons are useful bits of hardware that allow a standard guitar strap to be easily attached to your cigar box guitar. The image above shows a set of standard guitar strap buttons installed on one of our DIY guitar kits. There are other methods of doing this, and you don't even have to use an actual guitar strap. Builders have used all sorts materials as straps (old belts, purse straps, leather strips, braided cords, rope, etc.), and have attached them in all sorts of manners (screws, eye hooks, picture hanging hooks, etc.)

Adding a strap can make your instrument much easier to play while standing up, which is a concern of musicians who perform on stage. If your guitar will see some time on stage, definitely consider adding strap buttons and a strap!

Pickups

The topic of installing pickups on cigar box guitars could easily fill a dedicated book, and we can't really dig too deep into it here. But just as an overview, pickups are installed in your guitar and have an output jack, which allows the guitar to be plugged into an amplifier using a special cable.

The purpose of a pickup, jack and supporting wiring is to create an electrical circuit that "picks up" the vibrations of the instrument's strings, and conveys them to the amplifier (through an amp cable) so they can be heard.

There are many different types of guitar pickups, and one of the easiest to use is a disk-style piezoelectric pickup wired directly to an output jack. There are free articles over at CigarBoxGuitar.com that walk you through how to install one of these basic piezo & jack pickup harnesses in a cigar box guitar, as well various other types of pickups.

You can certainly choose to install a pickup into the cigar box guitar you build using this guide, but if you want my honest opinion, keeping your first build basic and simple is probably better. You will learn a lot through this process, and maybe make a mistake or two, and all of that experience can be carried forward into your next (probably more complex) build.

I wouldn't want you to bite off too much with your first attempt, to the point where you get frustrated and feel like giving up. Homemade instrument building works best when it is a gradual process where each instrument's creation builds on all of those that have gone before it.

Pickguards

Above: A reproduction of an acoustic guitar-style pickguard, attached to a 3-string cigar box guitar. This pickguard was cut from a 33 RPM LP record.

Pickguards are often seen on store-bought acoustic and electric guitars. On acoustic guitars they are usually placed below the central sound hole, in the area where the guitar pick tends to hit during heavy playing. On Electric guitars the sizes and shapes of pick guards vary, and in some cases they can cover a big chunk of the instrument's face.

You can certainly make a pickguard for your cigar box guitar, though many builders don't bother. In fact some, such as "King of the Cigar Box Guitar" Shane Speal, prefer the picking wear patterns that appear on the box lids over time as they are played.

Above: Shane Speal's classic Macanudo 3-string cigar box guitar, which he has been playing on stage for over twenty years. All of the wear seen on the sound board is from being played – no pick guards here!

Other Decorations and Embellishments

Many builders enjoy adding custom decorations to their cigar boxes. This covers a wide range of possibilities, beyond what we can get into here, but here is a list of ideas that you can use for inspiration. Kids especially enjoy decorating the box for what will be their very own cigar box guitar.

- Painting
- Stenciling
- Woodburning
- Stickers and decals

- Decoupage
- Laminating with printed materials: photos, newsprint, comic books, etc.
- Stamping
- Carving/etching (works best with high-end boxes that have solid wood panels)
- Electronics (installing LED lighting inside the box/mounted into the panel, etc.).

Here are some photos of some specially decorated cigar box guitars we have built over the years in the C. B. Gitty workshop, to inspire you as to some of the possibilities.

Above: An all-wood Cohiba cigar box has been custom-carved with a silhouette rendition of one of the few known photographs of Robert Johnson. After the carving was complete, black spraypaint was sprayed into it, and then sanded off of the uncarved surface once dry.

Above: A 3-string build with a box painted using a special water-dip method, creating a psychedelic color scheme.

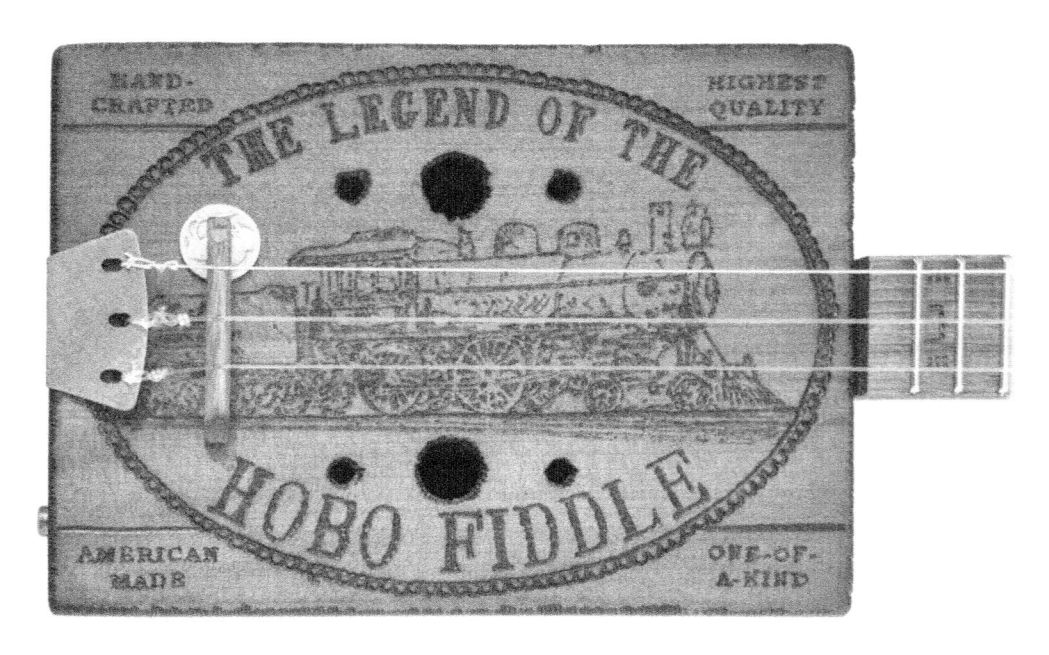

Above: One of the author's signature 3-string Hobo Fiddle® builds, with an original design wood-burned by hand into the top of the vintage all-wood cigar box.

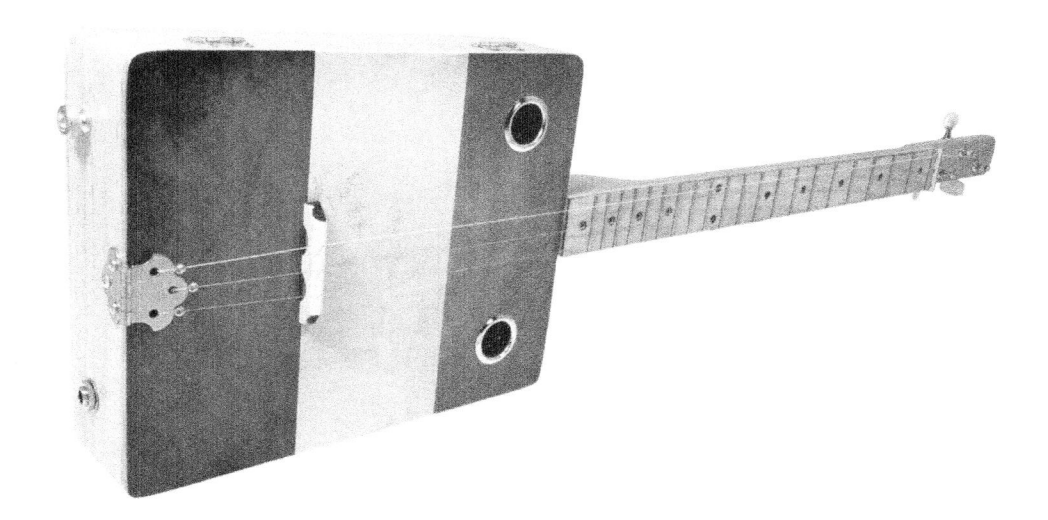

Above: A 3-string cigar box guitar with a specially printed soundboard featuring the tricolor flag of Ireland. The box was printed with a special flat-panel UV inkjet printer, but the same effect could be gotten with paint.

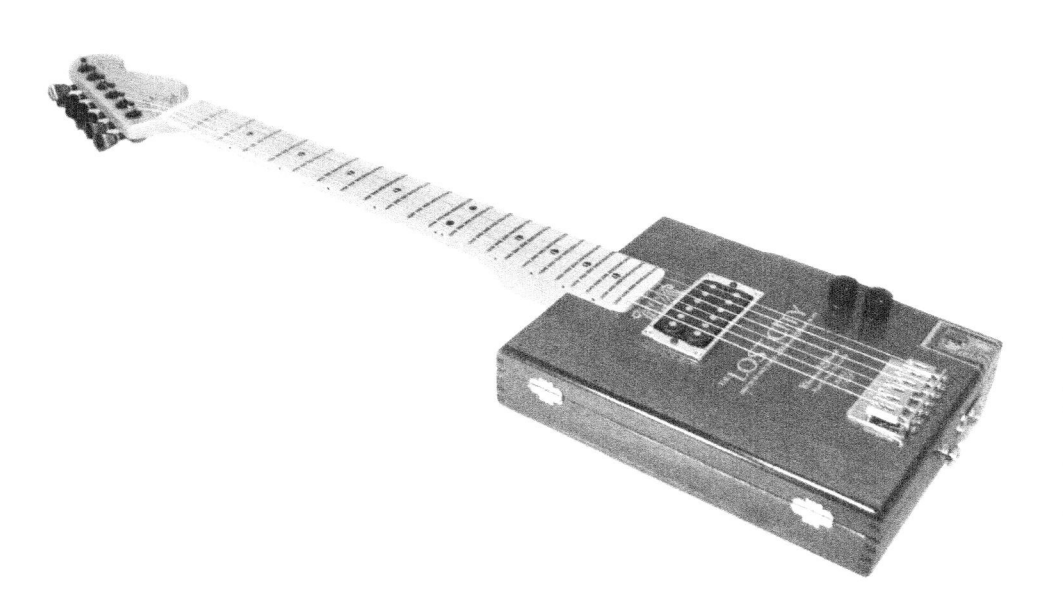

Above: This is definitely an advanced build! This cigar box guitar features a super premium Arturo Fuente Opus X "Lost City" solid wood cigar box, a Telecaster-style six-string electric guitar neck, a humbucker pickup and hard-tail bridge, and volume and tone controls. I include this here just as proof of the fact that you can make your CBGs just as fancy as you want to!

NOTES

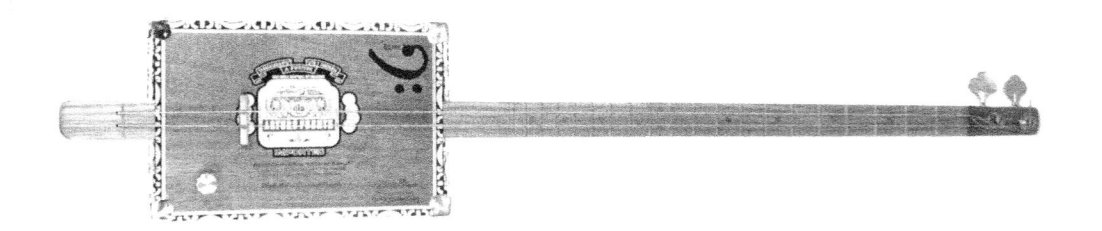

Above: This is a two-string cigar box bass guitar, using a big "Queen B" Arturo Fuente cigar box. Actually, though you can't really tell from this photo, this guitar used TWO of these cigar boxes, stacked one on top of the other and fastened together. These boxes are pretty thin, and using two of them made for a bass that was much more comfortable to hold and play.

Above: A Hobo Fiddle® three-string cigar box guitar/hybrid ukulele, built by the author. The cigar box is one of the all-wood "Corina Larks" vintage boxes mentioned earlier. Ben sanded the original branding off of the lid and woodburned in an original design featuring his fictional character "Three-String Sam" the Hobo. Woodburning on the box, neck and headstock can be a great way to add some unique flare to your cigar box guitars.

TOOLS

Now let's talk about the tools you'll need to build your first 3-string cigar box guitar. The good news is that only the most basic tools (and woodworking experience) are necessary to get the job done. Using only hand tools will work just fine, though you can upgrade to power tools if you have them available.

As mentioned earlier in this guide, be sure to follow all manufacturer safety recommendations when using your tools – eye, ear and lung protection are especially important.

SAW

A small, fine-toothed saw, such as a coping saw, hacksaw, keyhole saw or pull saw will be needed for cutting recesses into your neck, notching your cigar box, etc. The neck recessing can be greatly sped up if you have access to a bandsaw. A power scroll saw or hand-held jigsaw can also work for some of the cuts.

One word or warning from a lesson I learned the hard way: if you are using a handheld jigsaw (one where a straight blade extends from the bottom of the saw and moves up and down as you cut), and are cutting through the box lid to make sound holes or neck notches, make sure your fingers aren't in the path of the blade on the other side of what you are cutting!

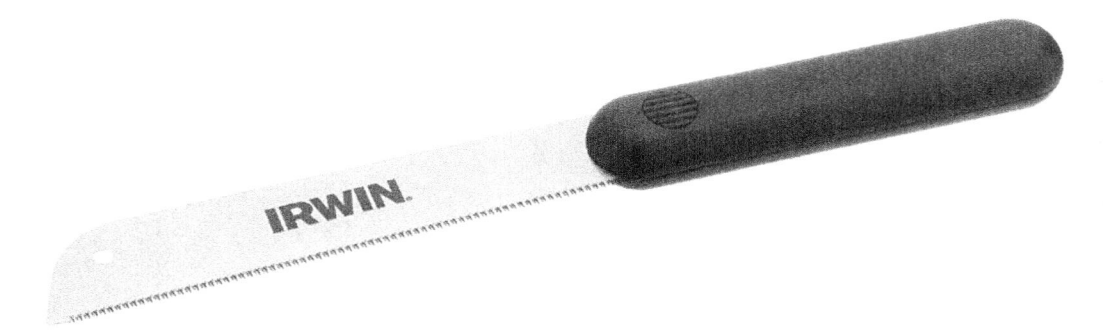

Above: A fine-toothed Irwin® brand pull saw (available from Amazon here: https://amzn.to/35D9o2I), is an inexpensive option for the cigar

box guitar builder, especially for the finer cuts required when cutting notches into the cigar box. However, the flexible blade makes it less useful for wider cuts (like neck recessing), as the blade can wander while sawing and cause uneven cuts.

DRILL

Either a hand drill (manual or power) or drill press will be needed for drilling tuner holes, sound holes and pilot holes for screws. A range of bit sizes (1/16", ¼", 5/16" and ½") are recommended.

If you are going to be using a hand drill, especially one that is the hand-crank style shown below, it is always recommended to pre-start your drill holes using a scratch awl, hole punch or the tip of a small fine-point Phillips screwdriver. Doing so will help keep the drill bit from wandering as you try to get the hole started, especially when using larger bits.

Also, when drilling tuner shaft holes, it is important to have the hole be perpendicular (at a 90-degree angle) to the headstock surface, which can be tricky when using a hand drill.

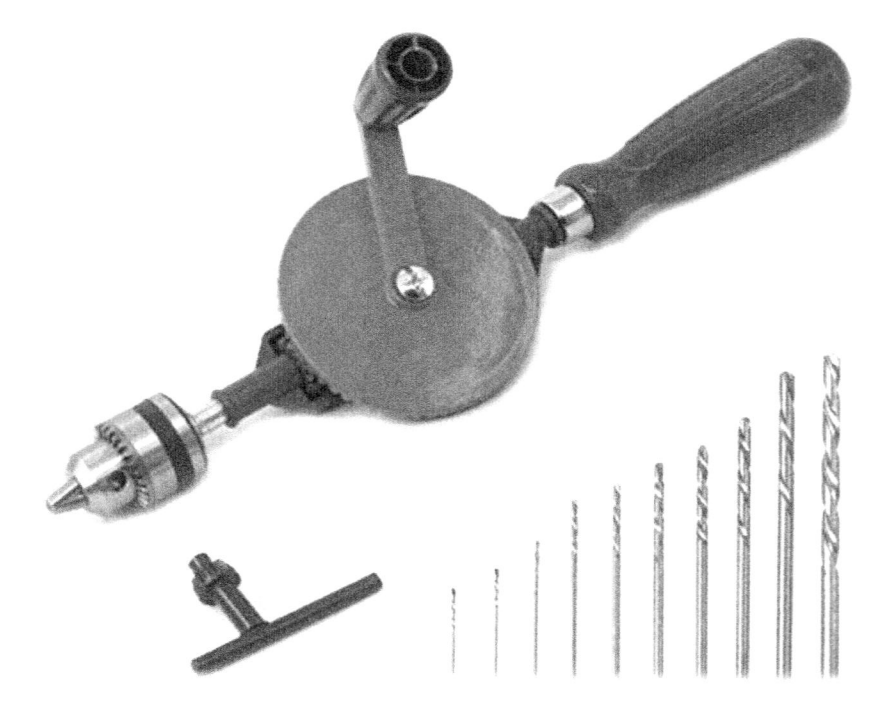

***Above:** A fairly inexpensive manual operation hand drill available from Amazon.*

SCREWDRIVER

A fine-point (#1 tip) Phillips screwdriver will be necessary for installing the tuner screws and potentially other smaller screws. A slightly larger-point screwdriver (#2 tip) may be better for any larger screws you need to install. A power screwdriver can be used, just be very careful if you are using it to install smaller screws – it is easy to go too far and twist off a screw head or strip out a hole.

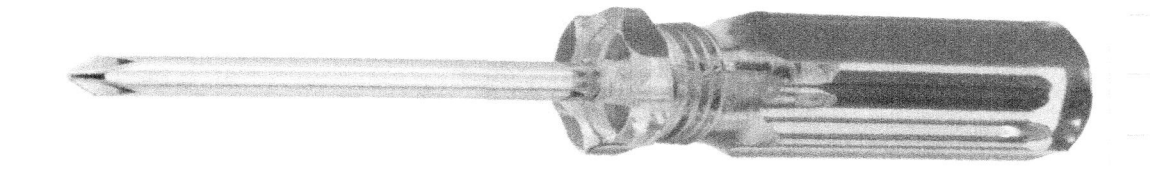

GLUE

You shouldn't need any glue for this project, unless you intend to be gluing in sound hole inserts. In that case, a hot glue gun is a great option, or you can use contact cement. Carpenter's or wood glue (Tite Bond, Elmer's, etc) is recommended for any time you want to glue two pieces of wood together – this shouldn't be necessary in building the guitar described in this guide, unless you have a wooden box and want to glue it shut.

Standard white or clear Elmer's brand school glue can also be handy for gluing paper borders back down if you are using paper-covered boxes. The decorative borders have a habit of coming loose, especially at the corners, and school glue works great to keep them in place.

WOOD FILE AND SANDPAPER

For optimum playing enjoyment, you'll want your CBG neck to be nice and smooth, and the only way to get that is by using sandpaper and possibly wood files and rasps. Rounding the back edges of the neck between the cigar box and the headstock can really improve the comfort level when playing, and for this purpose a rougher wood rasp is recommended.

NOTES

In general for shaping and smoothing operations, you start with rougher/coarser grits and work your way to finer grits for final sanding and polishing.

The amount of sanding and shaping you do on your cigar box guitar is entirely up to you. Having some sandpaper sheets ranging in grit from 80 up to 220 is recommended for any workshop. As for wood rasps and files, combo sets are available at most big-box hardware stores that include a range of styles.

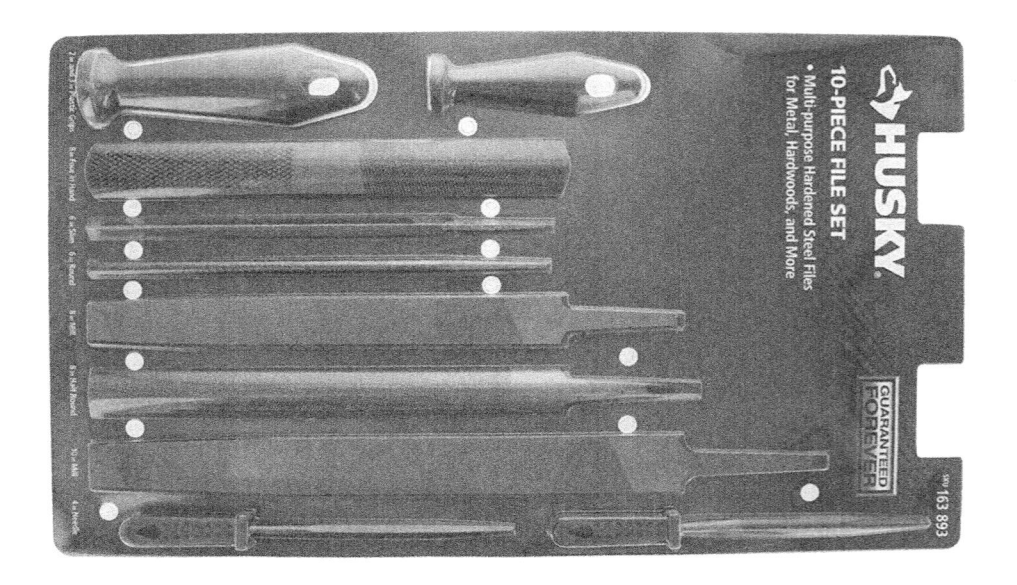

Above: A typical inexpensive file set that includes several styles of wood and metal files, including a double-ended wood rasp, which is very handy to have. You can find this particular set on Amazon using this link: https://amzn.to/33Mfl6S

RULER

You will need a ruler or measuring tape that can measure at least 25 inches (635mm) for getting your bridge in the right place. I recommend either a measuring tape or a yard (or meter) stick style ruler (36 inches /1 meter long).

OTHER TOOLS

A small hammer can be useful for tapping in tuner bushings and other "gentle encouragement" operations. If you are going to be doing any decorating, then of course other tools and supplies will be needed.

If you want to stain and finish your neck, you'll need brushes and rags and whatever else recommended by the manufacturer.

If you intend to glue pieces of wood together (not necessary if following the basic instructions in this guide) then you will need clamps to hold the pieces tightly together while the glue sets.

A set of nippers/side cutters is handy for trimming string ends to length, once they are installed.

A permanent marker is often used for marking fret positions on the bare cigar box guitar neck.

NOTES

Build Instructions

You've gathered your materials and tools, and prepared your workspace, and now you're ready to roll. Keep in mind as we proceed that these instructions show you how to build a "typical" basic three-string cigar box guitar using "typical" parts.

These instructions are based off the original how-to guide for the C. B. Gitty Basic 3-string CBG kit, which thousands of folks have used to build their first cigar box guitar.

Your build will very likely look different from my photos based on what parts you have sourced, and **you will likely need to tweak the instructions given below to fit the materials you have**. That is just part of the do-it-yourself reality, and no printed guide can cover every potential combination of parts and tools.

If your materials are very different from those shown in this guide, or you intend to venture off the "basic" path into more advanced areas, I strongly recommend reviewing the how-to materials at CigarBoxGuitar.com and the free plans at CigarBoxNation.com to learn more before proceeding. See the resources list at the end of this guide for specific links.

1. Prepare Your Workspace and Tools

Begin by preparing your work area and gathering the necessary tools as outlined above. Verify that you have all the parts you'll need. If you will be building your guitar on the dining room table or any other nicer surface, be sure to put down some cardboard or an old towel to protect it from scratches.

You will want a clear, flat area at least three feet long by a couple of feet wide to be able to comfortably build your guitar - but don't worry if you don't quite have that. Make do with what you do have, just be sure to keep safety in mind!

2. Cut the Neck to Length

Measure your neck and mark it for cutting at 34 inches from either end. When deciding where and how to cut it, look for any flaws, cracks, knots or other issues that you may be able to cut off and discard. A length of 34 inches is recommended, though a somewhat longer or shorter neck (+/- 2 inches) can work.

Once measured, use your hand or power saw to cut your neck to length. A light sanding can be done at this point, to remove any surface roughness as well as to clean up any rough-cut ends. This isn't the time to begin rounding off any corners or edges however, save that for Step 12 later.

3. Measure and Cut the Headstock Recess

Now take a look at your neck and decide which end you want to use as your headstock. Consider that the headstock and fingerboard will be the most visible part of the neck, compared to the section that goes through the box. So, if there are any interesting grain patterns in the wood, you might want them to be visible.

Also, if you have any small knots or other imperfections, you might be able to position them so that they are hidden inside the cigar box. This is entirely up to you - some builders like to have some imperfections visible on their builds to enhance the rustic nature.

Now grab your pencil and get ready to mark your head stock for the recess cutout, as shown in the photos below. The cutout should be **4 ½" long** and **¼" deep**. Be sure you mark your lines straight and square and always double-check all measurements before cutting. Refer to the photo below for a visual reference of how to measure and mare this.

Now, using a hand or power saw, cut the headstock recess according to the lines you've drawn, as shown below. Try to make this cut as smooth and even as possible, to reduce the amount of filing and sanding you'll have to do later.

Try to keep your cut as straight and smooth as possible - this will reduce filing and sanding later!

Above: The headstock recess has been marked, 4 ½ inches (114.3mm) long from the end of the neck, and ¼" (6.35mm) deep. Once marked and double-checked, you can proceed with cutting out the recess.

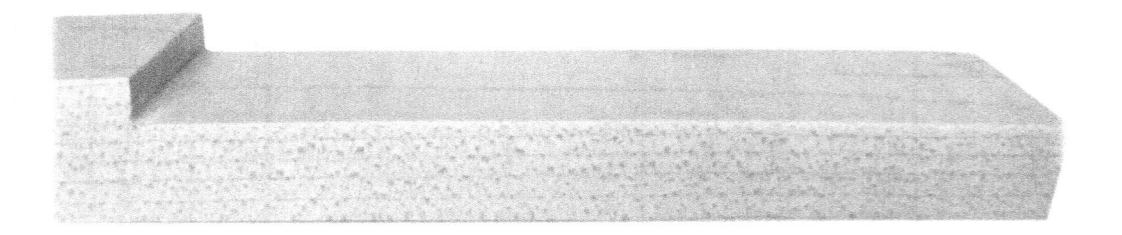

Above: A freshly cut headstock recess, ¼" (6.35mm) deep and 4 ½" (114.3mm) long.

4. Sand and Smooth the Headstock Cutout

Now it is time to finish and smooth the headstock cutout, which can take a little patience. Use a fine wood file to smooth out and remove the deeper saw marks, and then use progressively finer grades of sandpaper to make it baby smooth. If you don't have a wood file, just sandpaper will work with a little more elbow grease.

Of course, a power sander can make this job a snap, just be careful not to overdo it and thin down the headstock too much. You want it to remain as close as possible to ½" (12.7mm) thick to properly support the tuners.

If desired, you can leave the headstock rough for a more rustic look.

Above: Using a wood file to do the initial smoothing of the headstock recess, usually to be followed by fine-grit sandpaper (220 grit recommended) for final smoothing.

The photo below shows the finished headstock, ready for installation of the tuners.

Above: A fully smoothed and sanded headstock recess, ready for installation of tuners.

5. Mark Center Points of Cigar Box and Neck

Now it is time to mark your cigar box for the neck cutout. This will require some careful measuring and cutting to make sure everything will fit snugly.

The style of CBG you are building is called a "neck-through" style, where the neck extends all the way through the box. To allow this, two openings need to be cut into the box's end side panels, into which the neck will snugly fit. The process for marking and cutting these openings involves several steps, as illustrated in the photos below.

Please note that the measurements shown in these photos are specific to the cigar box being used; your box may be slightly smaller or larger, so be sure to measure carefully and do the calculations yourself. If your box has rounded edges, special accommodations may need to be made to find the center points.

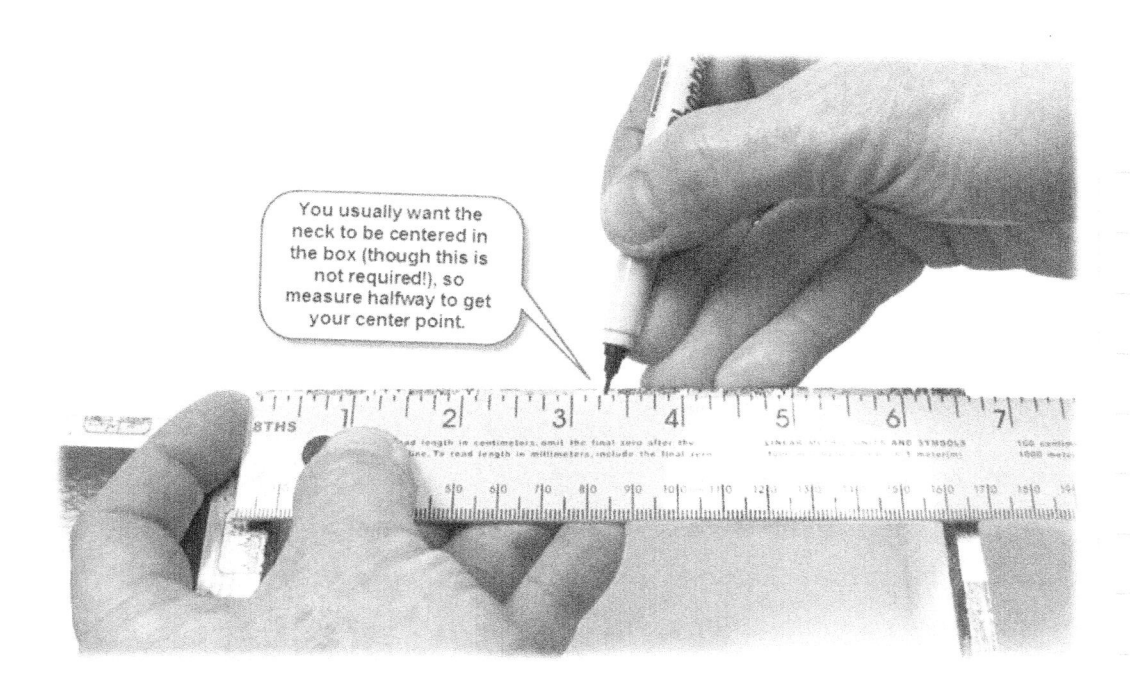

> You usually want the neck to be centered in the box (though this is not required!), so measure halfway to get your center point.

Above: Measuring and marking the center point of each end of your cigar box.

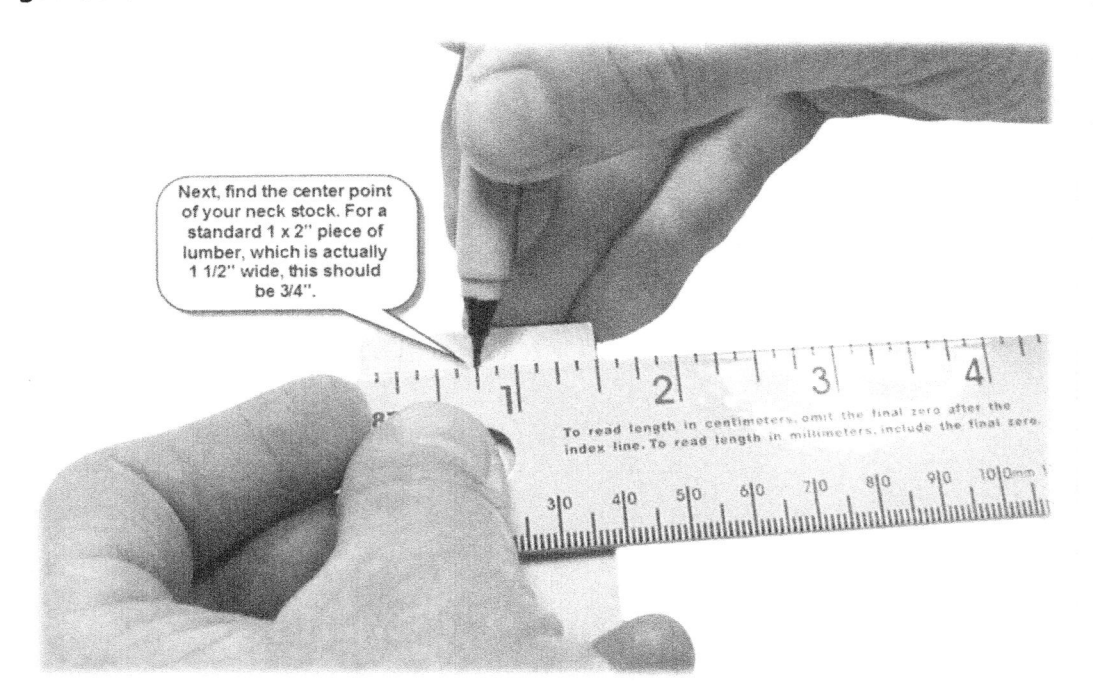

> Next, find the center point of your neck stock. For a standard 1 x 2" piece of lumber, which is actually 1 1/2" wide, this should be 3/4".

Above: Marking the center point of your neck. If using a standard "1 x 2" piece of lumber, it should be exactly 1 ½ inches wide, so your center point should be ¾-inch (0.75 inch / 19.05mm).

6. Mark the Neck Notches on the Cigar Box End Panels

It can be handy to use a scrap of 1 x 2 wood(such as the piece you may have cut off to get the neck length to 34 inches) for marking the box, but you can use the tail end of the neck itself instead. If you use the neck itself, it is recommended that you use pencil instead of a marker, so that any marks left on the sides of the neck can be more easily removed later.

PRO TIP: If you are using a paper-covered cigar box such as the one shown in these photos, it can be a good idea to put blue painter's tape over the paper on the ends before marking the notches, and leave it on through the cutting process. This tape can help protect the paper and keep it from ripping while sawing.

Above: Using a scrap cutoff or the end of the neck itself to mark a rectangular notch on each end of the cigar box.

Above: The neck notch marked on the end of the cigar box. This should be done on both ends, to allow a path for the neck to fully extend through the box.

Once you have marked both sides of your box, it is time to cut the openings. It is recommended that you use a small saw (such as a coping saw or the Irwin® brand pull-saw pictured previously) for this, but make do the best you can with what you have.

It is always better to cut the opening a little on the small side on the first cut, as you can always enlarge it later with a file. You want your neck to fit as snugly as possible into these notch openings.

7. Cut the Neck Notches into the Cigar Box

The photos below show how you first make the straight side cuts, and then use a two-cut method to cut the bottom. If your saw has a wider blade that can't cut curves, you can achieve the same effect by making several angled cuts.

PRO TIP: For paper-covered boxes with sides made from MDF/hardboard, multiple passes with a box cutter/razor knife can also be used to cut the edges of the notches. Each pass cuts a little deeper until you are through – just be careful not to cut yourself using this method!

Above: Beginning one of the neck notch cutouts. Please note that while these photos do not show any blue painter's tape in place, applying some before marking and cutting can help protect the paper on this style of cigar box.

Above: After making both vertical cuts, make a curved (or angled) cut that meets the further vertical cut.

Above: Finish by joining the cuts to remove the angled/curved portion.

Repeat this process on both ends. Once you are finished cutting, test the fit of your neck, and if necessary use a fine-cut wood file to carefully enlarge the cutouts. Ideally, you want the neck to fit very snugly and to be flush with the top of the cigar box

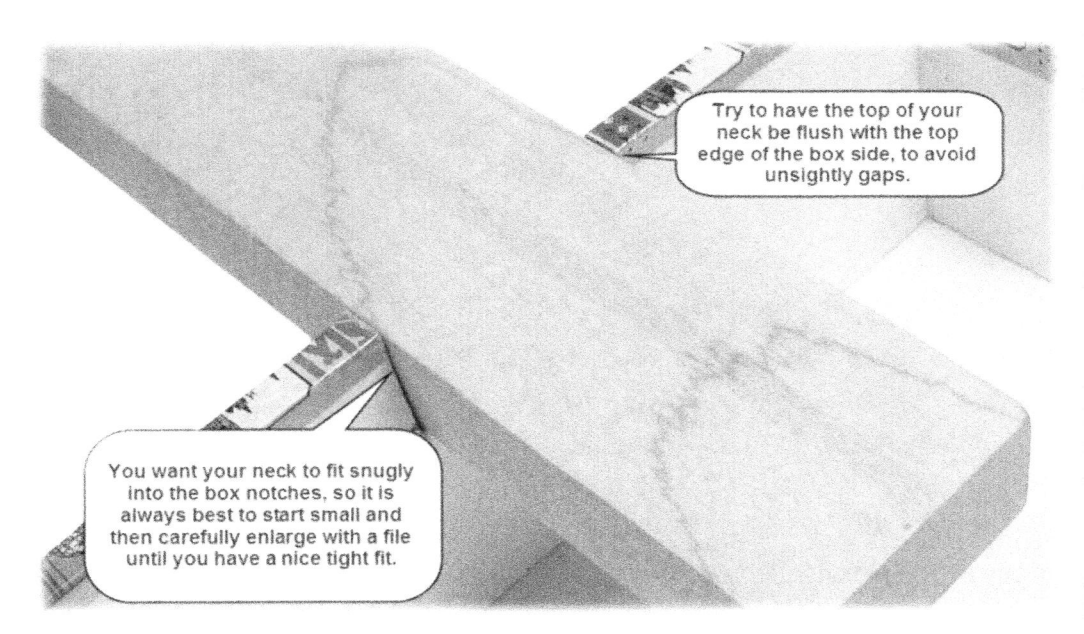

Above: A neck snugly fit into a freshly cut notch.

Above: A box properly notched and ready for determination of neck placement.

8. Determining Neck Placement in the Box

With your neck notches cut, the next step is to figure out the exact neck placement within the box. This involves a little bit of figuring, but nothing too heavy.

You will want a couple of inches of neck sticking out the bottom of the box to form a tailpiece heel, and you will want your bridge to be about two or three inches from the edge of the box, for the best sound. If you started with a neck shorter than the recommended 34 inches, then your heel may be shorter – as long as it is about an inch you should be OK.

To achieve this, place the neck in the notches such that about 2 1/8" sticks out the bottom, as shown in the picture above, and you should be fine. Make sure that the long part of the neck extends out of the correct side, so that the artwork on the front of the cigar box will be right-side-up when you are holding the instrument in playing position.

***PRO TIP:** For building a left-handed cigar box guitar, you would want* *the neck sticking out the opposite way as what will be shown through the remainder of the photos in this guide. All of the other steps remain the same.*

9. Mark the Neck for Box Recess Cut

In order to allow the cigar box lid to close over the neck where it passes through, we will need to cut a recess down into the wood of the neck, just a bit deeper than the thickness of the lid. The reason we cut deeper than the actual thickness is so a space is left to keep the lid from resting against the neck, which would dampen the instrument's acoustic sound.

To proceed, use a straight-edge to mark the neck on the **inside** edges of the box. These marks will be used in cutting out the box lid recess, as shown in the series of pictures that follow. The explanatory bubbles in the photos will help to walk you through the steps.

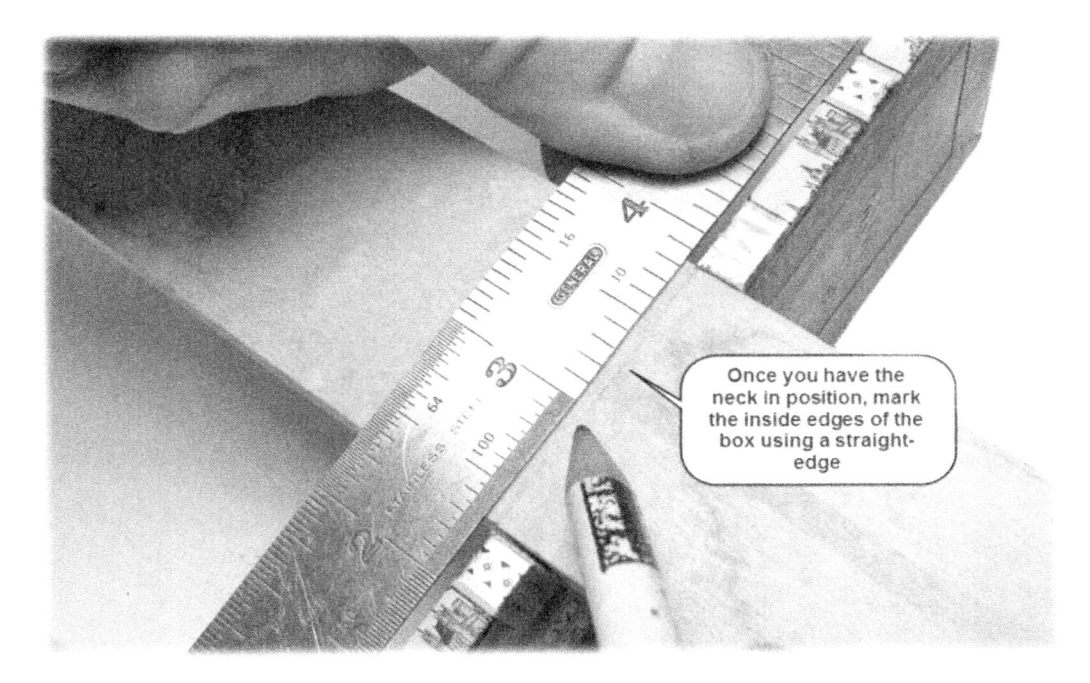

Above: Marking a straight line on the neck along the INSIDE edge of the cigar box's end panels. These will form the end points of the box lid neck recess. Carefully extend these lines down over the sides of the neck at an exact 90-degree angle.

A leftover piece from the neck cutout makes a great guide for determining the depth of the neck's box lid recess. We recommend giving it about 1/8" extra, so there is some air space between the box lid and the neck recess.

Above: If your cigar box's lid is the same thickness as the side panels, you can use one of the pieces you cut out in the previous steps as a depth guide for cutting the neck recess. Otherwise, you will need to use a ruler to measure the lid thickness and mark a notch of appropriate depth – usually about 1/16-inch (0.0625 in. / 1.6mm) deeper than the lid thickness.

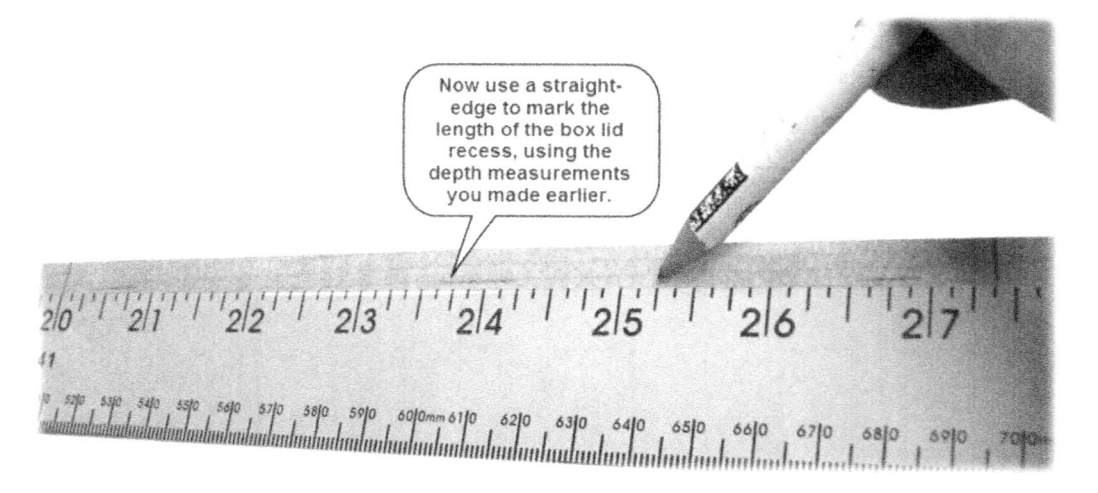

Now use a straight-edge to mark the length of the box lid recess, using the depth measurements you made earlier.

Above: Having marked the inside edges of the box, and determined the cutout depth needed based on lid thickness, use your straight edge to draw the notch's bottom line as a guide for sawing.

In general, if using a 3/4-inch thick 1 x 2 as your neck, try not to make the total depth of your neck recess any deeper than ¼-inch (0.25 in. /

6.35mm). Or in other words, try to leave at least 1/2-inch (0.50 in. / 12.7mm) of neck wood to go through the box. You want to make sure there is enough of the neck left to support the tension of the strings.

PRO TIP: Leaving the lid notch a little higher at each end, or sawing in a sort of "stair step" there, so that the neck just barely touches the underside of the lid, can help hold the neck firmly in place with no movement. See the diagram below for a visual.

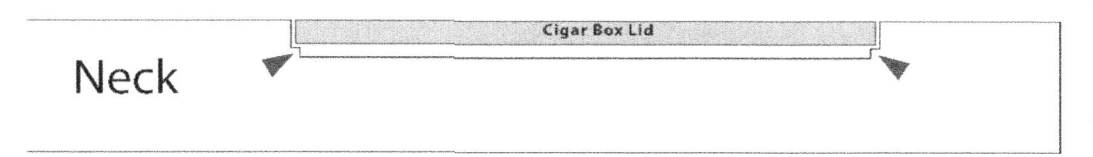

Above: Leaving small raised steps on each end of the box lid notch in the neck can help support the lid and keep the neck more firmly held in place once mounted in the box. Sawing a slight upward curve into each end can have the same result.

10. Cut the Neck Recess

Be sure that the neck recess markings are straight and square, then use your saw to cut it out. Make the vertical end cuts first (cutting on the INSIDE edges of the lines), then ease into the cut at one end with a curve. Once that cut is complete, cut out the remaining piece at the other end.

Try your best to keep the long cut along the bottom edge as smooth and even as possible, to reduce the amount of sanding and filing you'll need to do in the next step.

Be careful that your saw blade doesn't "wander" across the width, especially on the side facing away from you while cutting. Depending on the type of saw you are using, sometimes a cut can wander off course quite a bit from one side of a wide cut to the other, and you'll end up with a much shallower or deeper cut on one side.

NOTES

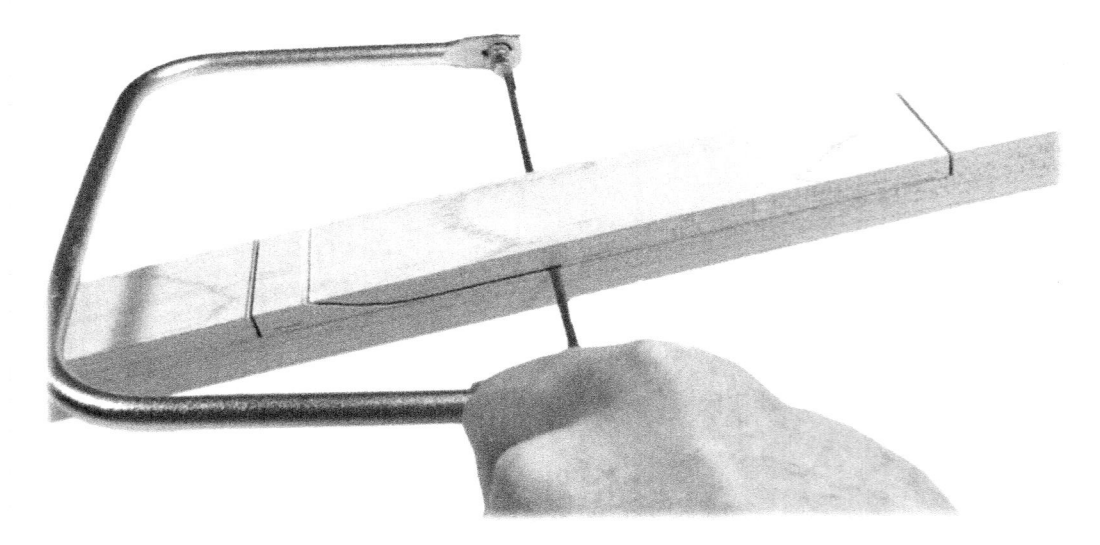

Above: Using a coping saw to cut the neck notch. The end cuts are made first and then the long horizontal cut. A final step after the cut above is finished will be to go back and cut out the remaining piece behind the curved entry cut.

When you are finished cutting the recess, do some initial leveling and smoothing with your wood file, to take down any raised or uneven areas.

Now, insert the neck into the box and try to close the lid. You want a nice snug fit between the lid edge and the sides of the recess cut out. If the lid won't close, use your wood file to square up and enlarge the opening as necessary, until the lid fits very snugly into it, as shown in the photo below.

Note that with this style of CBG, the neck is held in place purely by friction, and you shouldn't need to use glue or other methods to fasten it in place.

> If necessary, use a flat file to carefully enlarge your box lid recess until the lid fits very snugly into it. Always start smaller and carefully enlarge!

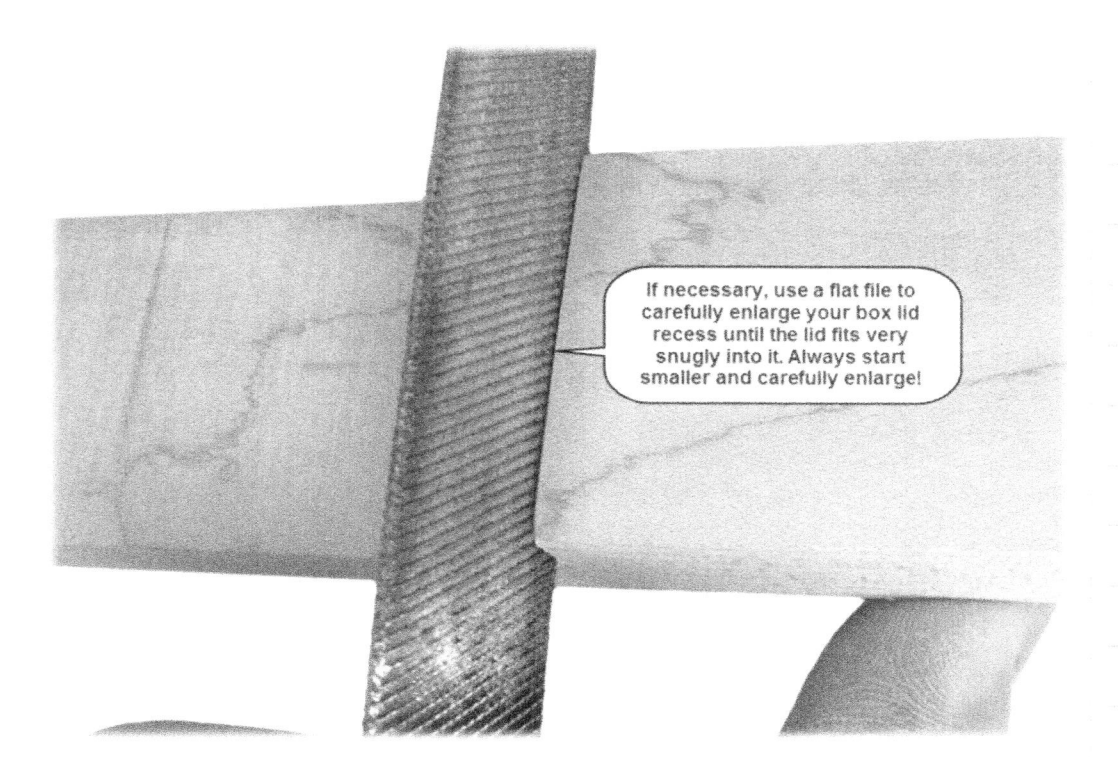

Above: Using a wood file to square up and slightly enlarge the box lid neck notch recess. While this can seem tedious, remember that it is much easier to make an opening a little larger via filing than it is to try to fix/cover an opening that has been cut too big. The length of your neck notch, which finished, should be almost exactly the same (just a hair over) the length of your cigar box's lid, so that the lid will down into it fairly tightly.

Did You Know...

Lightnin' Hopkins, one of the founding fathers of the Blues, built a cigar box guitar as his first instrument. In his own words: *"So I went ahead and made me a guitar. I got me a cigar box, I cut me a round hole in the middle of it, take me a little piece of plank, nailed it onto that cigar box, and I got me some screen wire and I made me a bridge back there and raised it up high enough that it would sound inside that little box, and got me a tune out of it. I kept my tune and I played from then on."*

NOTES

Above: The neck should fit evenly and snugly into the neck notches cut into the cigar box, and the lid edge should be nice and tight against the sides of the lid notch.

Above: Your neck should fit nice and tight into the cigar box.

Depending on how deep you made your neck notch, and how tight the fit is, you might notice that your neck moves up and down a little bit in the box notches with the lid closed – especially if you didn't leave raised areas as advised above.

If this is the case, you can glue in a shim or two at either end of the neck notch, which the box lid will press against when closed to keep the neck from moving around. A layer or two of wooden toothpicks or popsicle sticks laid across the width of the neck can work well for this.

11. Prepping and Installing the Tailpiece

In this section I'll show you two different tailpiece methods. The first doesn't require a separate piece of hardware, and instead uses the neck heel itself as the tailpiece/anchoring point. The second method uses a small metal hinge as a tailpiece, which some builders prefer.

Neck Heel String Anchoring

To use this method, basically you will be drilling three small holes - usually 1/16-inch (0.0625 in. / 1.6mm) to 3/32-inch (0.09375 in. / 2.4mm) in diameter – in the heel part of the neck that extends from the bottom end of the cigar box.

The strings will be fed up through these holes and then run across the box, over the bridge, and up the neck. The ball ends of the strings will not fit through the drilled holes, and will be anchored in place once the string tension is increased.

This is a simple and straightforward method, and generally works well, although some builders don't like the aesthetics of it. The two photos below show this method in use on a CBG built by Shane Speal.

TOP VIEW   **BOTTOM VIEW**

Above: One method of anchoring the strings via holes drilled in the neck heel. This removes the need for a separate piece of hardware to use as a tailpiece.

Some builders will insert string ferrules into the drilled holes to dress them up a bit, and also to keep the strings from biting into the wood, but this is entirely optional.

Hinge Tailpiece Method

If you have chosen to use a hinge as your tailpiece, now it is time to prepare it for mounting. There are two ways you can go about this: drilling string holes in your hinge, or using the holes already there.

The harder and (usually) more elegant method is to drill new holes in your hinge, one for each string. If you go this route, use a 1/16" or 3/32" drill bit to drill the string holes, as shown in the photo below.

Be careful while drilling through the metal, especially if using a hand drill, as it can be pretty tricky. The thicker the metal of the hinge, the harder it will be to drill through it, and the hotter your bit (and the hinge) will get as you drill. The bit may also want to grab and bind with the metal, causing the hinge to spin, which can do a number on your fingers.

You should use a clamp of some sort to hold the hinge in place against your bench top or a piece of scrap wood while drilling, and if possible use a punch or an old fine-point Phillips screwdriver you don't care too much about to create a starter divot where you want the hole. This helps keep the drill bit from "walking" as you are trying to get the drill bit started.

The exact hole position will vary depending on the type of hinge you are using, but in general having them be about ½-inch (12.7mm) apart works well.

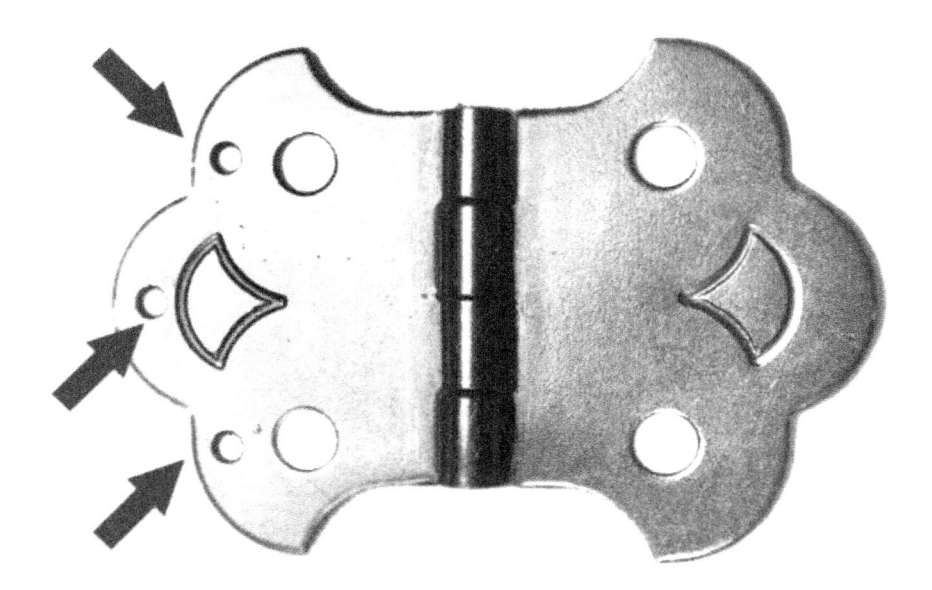

Above: A typical brass-plated hinge drilled with three new string holes.

After drilling, some rough edges and burrs may be left around the hole edge on the back side of the hinge – use a small metal file or sandpaper to remove these, as they can be rather sharp.

Once you are done drilling, mount your tailpiece hinge on the end of the neck as shown in the photos that follow. Note that the screws go into the under-side of the neck. Be sure to pre-drill the screw holes before inserting screws!

Depending on the type of hinge you used, the original mounting holes might not line up quite right with your neck. You may need to drill new

NOTES

holes or get creative to get it properly mounted. Don't worry if it doesn't look exactly like the photos below, just make sure that your strings will be able to be cleanly strung through it and run over the box and up the neck.

Above: For this style of hinge, the mounting screws are installed up into the bottom of the neck, so that the other side of the hinge will just barely protrude over the top rim of the neck. You could also mount it such that the screws go into the very end of the neck and the hinge bends over the top of it.

Above: The hinge tailpiece mounted to the neck. Note that the sharp metal burrs on the drilled string holes have not yet been filed off.

12. Drill the Sound Holes

Sound holes play an important role in any acoustic stringed instrument, including your soon-to-be cigar box guitar: in short, they let the sound out. While a CBG without them will still make sound, it is pretty much guaranteed to be fuller and richer in volume and tone if there are some sound holes drilled into the cigar box lid (which from now on I will start calling the "sound board").

There aren't any hard-and-fast rules when it comes to sound hole number, size or placement, but there are some general guidelines. Usually for a cigar box guitar a single sound hole about one inch (25.4mm) in diameter is sufficient.

On store-bought acoustic guitars we're used to seeing the sound hole in the center, but on a neck-through instrument like this you can't really put one there because the neck would be directly under it and it wouldn't be as effective. As such, many builders drill their sound holes on either side of the neck, usually towards the top half of the box (towards the headstock), but even that can vary.

If you don't have a one-inch bit for your drill (usually only hole saws, Forstner bits and spade bits go up that large), you can instead drill several smaller holes. In the images that follow, we'll be drilling four ½-inch (12.7mm) holes, and then gluing screened grommets into the holes.

Remember that if you don't have grommets, you can leave the holes bare – though you might want to gently sand around their edges (or use a sharp razor blade) to remove any lingering bits of wood or paper, and you can also use a black marker to darken the inside edges of the holes so they don't stand out quite so much.

To proceed, use a ½-inch or 5/8-inch bit to drill the holes. If you intend to install grommets and are using a ½-inch bit, you may need to jiggle the bit around a bit while drilling to enlarge the holes a little more, to get them to fit correctly. You can also use a round wood file to enlarge the holes slightly.

Note that you don't have to drill the sound holes in the locations shown in this guide, and you don't have to have four of them! There are a lot of different theories out there about what the "best" sound hole set up is for a Cigar Box Guitar.

There is no reason to get too worried about it though – in general, three or four ½-inch sound holes will be fine for a CBG of this size.

Above: Drilling sound holes in the cigar box guitar lid.

Once your holes are drilled, test the fit of the grommets (if using them), and enlarge the holes if necessary. Then use a multipurpose glue or a hot glue gun to set the grommets into the holes. Be careful to not get glue on the surface of your box! Many find it easier to hold the grommets in place and glue from the inside.

The photos that follow show the prepped box with sound holes drilled and optional grommet inserts glued into place.

NOTES

Above: Our cigar box with its sound holes drilled and optional grommet inserts glued into place. We are now ready to proceed with the remaining steps of building the guitar.

Above: A close-up of the screened grommet sound hole insert glued into place.

Below are example photos of some other cigar box guitars we have built in the C. B. Gitty shop, with various sound hole configurations to give you some inspiration and ideas.

Above: A single large sound hole above the neck. The screened sound hole insert shown here is the same style used on Dobro® resonators and some steel guitars. They are available from C. B. Gitty in chrome, gold and black.

Above: On this CBG we used an array of smaller sound holes set with 15mm screened brass grommets.

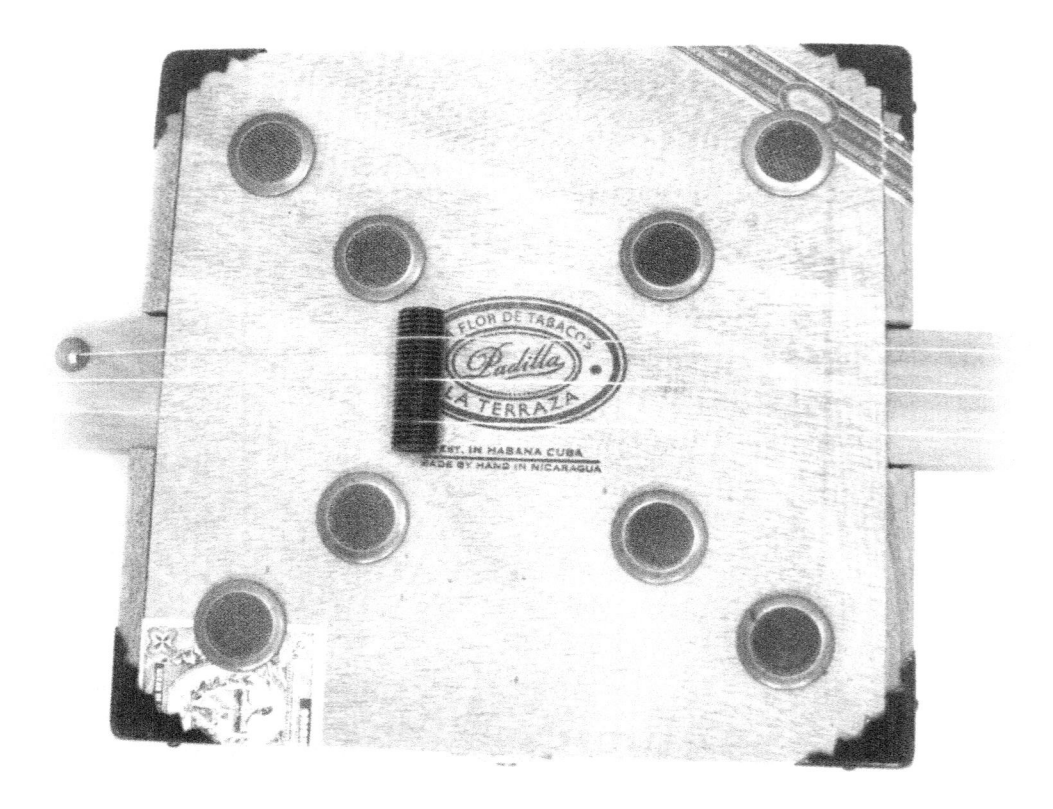

Above: This square-bodied cigar box guitar seemed right for an "X" sound hole pattern. While technically this is more sound holes than a guitar this size should need, sometimes aesthetics win out over technical requirements.

Did You Know...

Back in 2011 or so, Johnny Depp gave Paul McCartney his favorite cigar box guitar, which happened to be a four-string "Cig Fiddle" built by Matty Baratto. Paul played his CBG during the 12.12.12 hurricane benefit concert and also on Saturday Night Live later the same week. In 2014, Sir Paul and his cigar box guitar joined Dave Grohl and the other surviving members of Nirvana, and recorded a track "Cut Me Some Slack" which went on to win a Grammy award that same year. This is the only Grammy-winning song where the lead was played on a cigar box guitar.

Above: Another multi sound hole pattern, mixing larger and smaller holes set with screened grommets.

Above: A single larger sound hole covered with a surface-mount cover. C. B. Gitty carries a range of designs of this type of sound hole cover.

Above: An interesting treatment of sound holes decorated to make them look like bullet holes, on a rustic western-themed CBG.

13. Do Final Shaping/Sanding of Neck and Apply Finish (Optional)

This is the best time to do any rounding of the back of the neck, as well as the neck heel and headstock. It much easier to do this before the tuners are installed (but after their positions are marked, and before the neck is mounted into the box. If you decide to shape the headstock, hold your tuners up to it first to get an idea of the space they will take up, so you don't sand away too much wood.

If you do want to round off the back corners of the neck, make a mark about half an inch above where the neck will meet the cigar box when in final position, and only round the neck off up to that point. Don't round the corners where it will enter the cigar box, otherwise you will end up with unsightly gaps between the rounded neck edges and the square corners of the box's neck notches.

If you want to apply some sort of finish to your CBG neck, this would be a good time to do it. Whether a simple rub-on option like linseed or Danish oil, or something fancier involving staining and varnish or polyurethane, the finish is entirely up to you.

For the build in the photos, we chose to just leave the wood natural and unfinished. It is recommended that if you are going to apply a finish, you do so before installing the tuners - you don't want anything to gum up their gears.

14. INSTALL THE TUNERS/MACHINE HEADS

Installation of the tuners is not difficult, but it does need to be done right - so follow the instructions in the photos below carefully and you shouldn't have any trouble. Note that the brass gear on the backs of the tuners should always be towards the BODY of the instrument when mounted, not towards the top of the neck. With some varieties of tuners, the gears are not visible because they are covered or housed in the tuner body - see the photos that follow the one below for a visual reference.

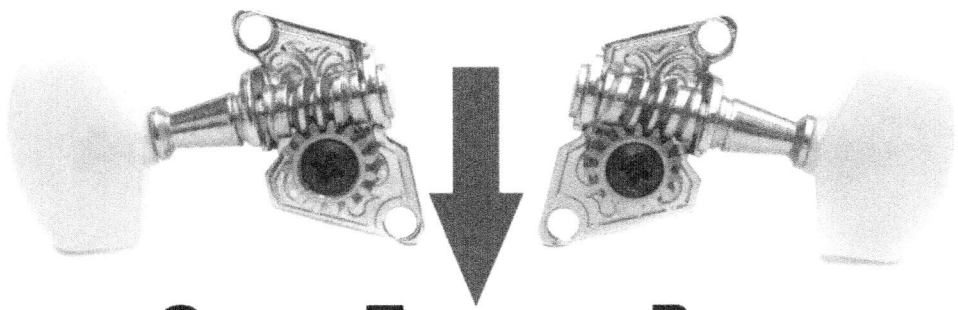

GEARS TOWARDS BODY

Above: A diagram showing how tuners should be mounted. Note when installing tuners that references to "left" and "right" refers to what side they should be mounted on when looking at the BACK of the headstock (the side that is facing towards you when you are actually installing the tuners).

NOTES

Above: A "sealed-gear" style of tuner, with the gear housed inside the tuner body in the rounded portion referred to by the arrow. This rounded portion should be oriented towards the body of the instrument when the tuner is mounted in the headstock.

Above: "Covered-gear" tuners have a stamped metal plate that covers the gears. Usually these covers can be removed before installation if need be. The tuners shown above have the gears oriented downwards.

Above: Some tuners are designed as "three on a plate", and must be mounted in-line. The gears should still be oriented towards the body of the instrument. Note that with this style of tuner, you have to be very certain to get the shaft holes in the right spots. Here's a trick: with a lead pencil, use the side of the sharpened lead to rub the end of each shaft, and then touch it to the headstock along the 3/8" line you've drawn (see instructions below). This should leave a faint gray mark to indicate where each hole should be drilled.

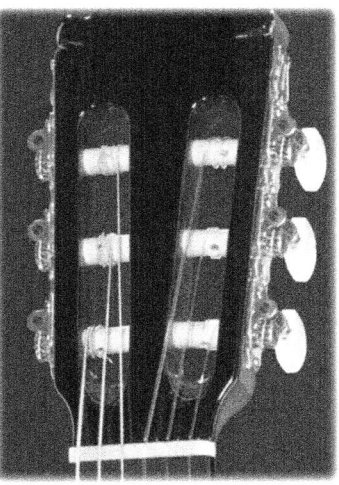

Above: Three-on-a-plate classical guitar-style tuners, with thicker ceramic or plastic shafts. These are meant to be mounted from the SIDE of the headstock, with the shafts (and string holes) extending into a slot cut down the face of the headstock. Using these tuners is a more advanced task. The image to the right above shows how they are installed on a conventional six string classical nylon-string guitar.

Determining Your Tuner Alignment

The first thing to do before making any marks or drilling any holes is to figure out the alignment of your tuners. Set them on the table in front of you aligned the same as was shown in the "Gears Towards Body" photo above. There are four possibilities of what you will have: two left & one right; two right & one left; all three left; or all three right. Any of these combinations will work, but you will have to alter the layout of the tuner holes shown in the images that follow to match what you have.

For reference, the photos that follow will show the holes being laid out and drilled for a TWO LEFT / ONE RIGHT configuration. For two right / one left, just reverse what is shown – remembering that in this instance, "right" and "left" refers to which side the tuners go on when looking at the BACK of the headstock, and with the gear portion of the tuners oriented towards the body of the instrument.

If you have a set of all three left or all three right tuners, then you'll be drilling a line of three holes on one side of the headstock or the other. Just make sure that the holes are spaced far enough apart that the tuner buttons won't be too close together, which makes them hard to turn. Use the hole-marking trick described in the photo caption above to help get it right.

Marking Tuner Hole Location

The diagram below shows the layout of where the holes will be drilled for tuners in a two left / one right configuration.

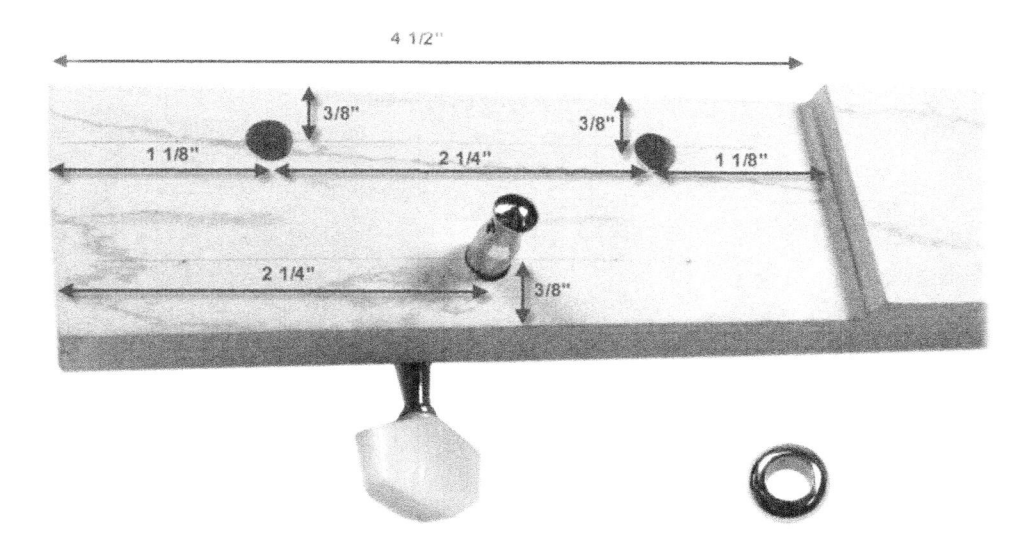

Above: The recommended headstock drilling layout for tuners in a two left /one right configuration. For two right / one left, this would be reversed. For three-left or three-right, all three holes would be on one side of the headstock or the other. Note that these measurements are all intended to be "center to center" even though a couple of the arrows don't point to the exact center of the holes shown.

To mark your headstock for this layout, begin by measuring in 3/8-inch (0.375 inch / 9.5mm) from each edge, and make light marks with a pencil.

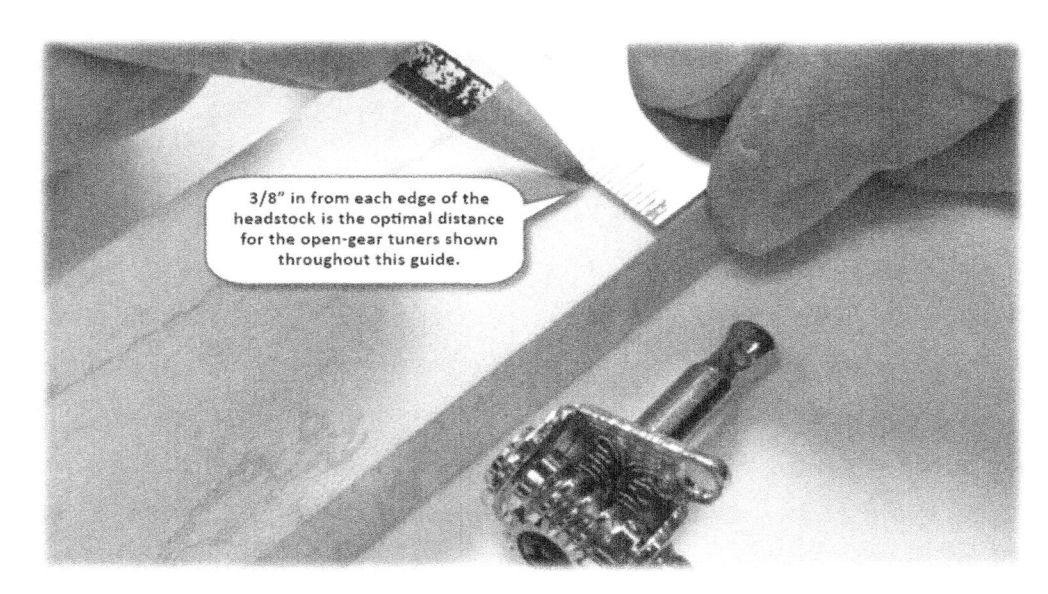

Above: Measure in 3/8-inch (0.375 in. / 9.5mm) from each edge of the headstock to get the offset position for the tuners. This will allow the tuner buttons to stick out just the right amount.

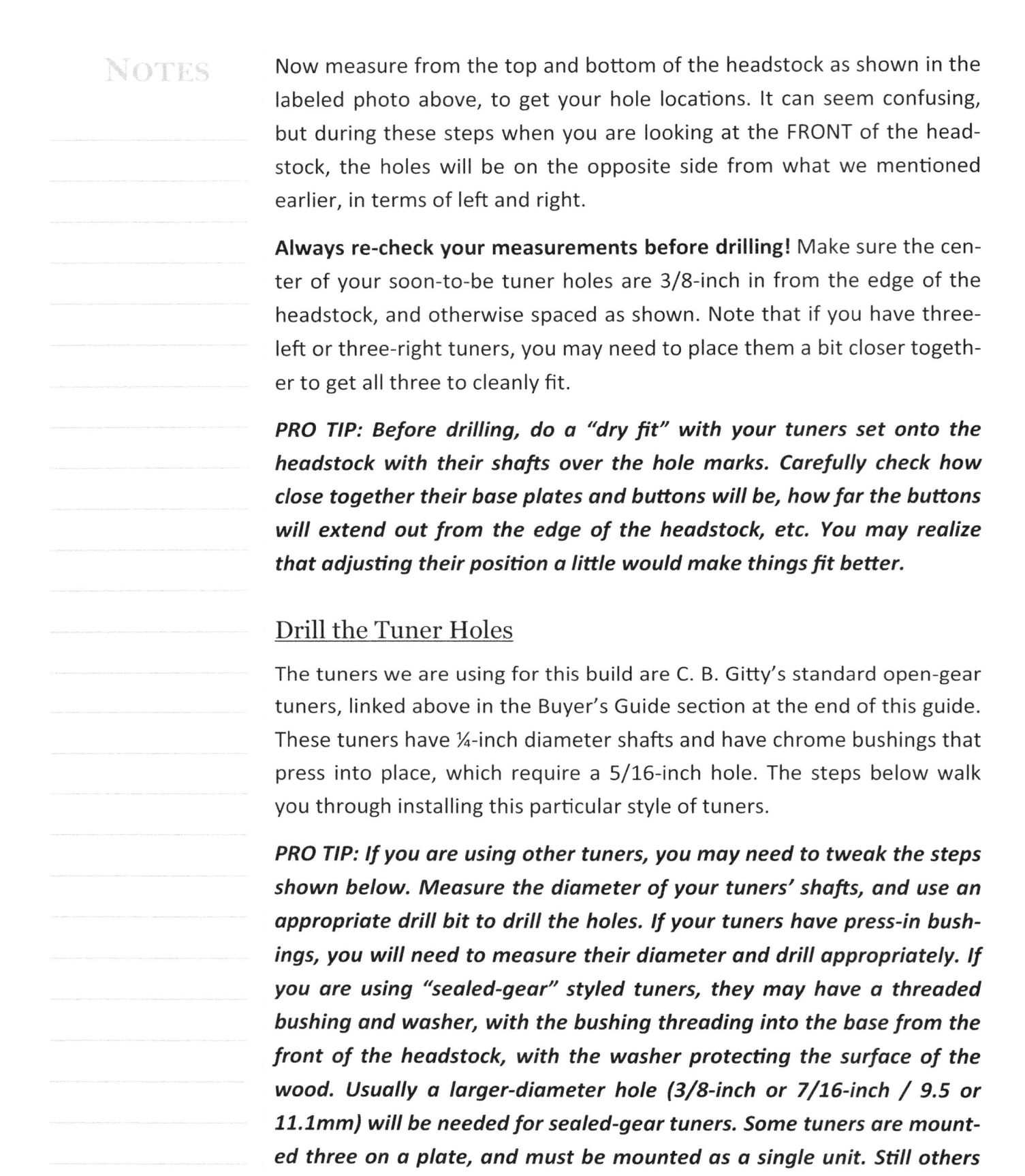

Now measure from the top and bottom of the headstock as shown in the labeled photo above, to get your hole locations. It can seem confusing, but during these steps when you are looking at the FRONT of the headstock, the holes will be on the opposite side from what we mentioned earlier, in terms of left and right.

Always re-check your measurements before drilling! Make sure the center of your soon-to-be tuner holes are 3/8-inch in from the edge of the headstock, and otherwise spaced as shown. Note that if you have three-left or three-right tuners, you may need to place them a bit closer together to get all three to cleanly fit.

PRO TIP: Before drilling, do a "dry fit" with your tuners set onto the headstock with their shafts over the hole marks. Carefully check how close together their base plates and buttons will be, how far the buttons will extend out from the edge of the headstock, etc. You may realize that adjusting their position a little would make things fit better.

Drill the Tuner Holes

The tuners we are using for this build are C. B. Gitty's standard open-gear tuners, linked above in the Buyer's Guide section at the end of this guide. These tuners have ¼-inch diameter shafts and have chrome bushings that press into place, which require a 5/16-inch hole. The steps below walk you through installing this particular style of tuners.

PRO TIP: If you are using other tuners, you may need to tweak the steps shown below. Measure the diameter of your tuners' shafts, and use an appropriate drill bit to drill the holes. If your tuners have press-in bushings, you will need to measure their diameter and drill appropriately. If you are using "sealed-gear" styled tuners, they may have a threaded bushing and washer, with the bushing threading into the base from the front of the headstock, with the washer protecting the surface of the wood. Usually a larger-diameter hole (3/8-inch or 7/16-inch / 9.5 or 11.1mm) will be needed for sealed-gear tuners. Some tuners are mounted three on a plate, and must be mounted as a single unit. Still others (classical style) are meant from mounting from the side through an elongated slot cut through the headstock. Photos of these styles were previously shown, review them if needed.

With your holes marked and measurements double-checked, use a ¼" drill bit to drill the tuner holes. Make sure that the drill bit is perfectly perpendicular to the headstock when drilling (in other words, not angled) so that the holes are at a true 90-degree angle to the surface. Angled holes can force tuner shafts off center and cause gears to slip.

***PRO TIP:** For the C. B. Gitty open-gear tuners shown in these steps, some builders will just drill all the way through the headstock with a 5/16-inch bit, and rely on the bushings to hold the tuner shaft exactly centered. It usually works just fine. Whether you do that, or do the two-step drilling described below, is up to you.*

Once you have the ¼" holes drilled for the tuner shafts, you will need to drill the top half of the holes slightly wider for the tuner bushings. A 5/16-inch drill bit is necessary to drill the bushing holes. It is highly recommended that you use a piece of tape on the drill bit as a depth gauge to keep from going go all the way through the headstock - though as mentioned in the Pro Tip above, it's not the end of the world if you do. Drill them just deep enough to accept the tuner bushings, as shown in the photo below.

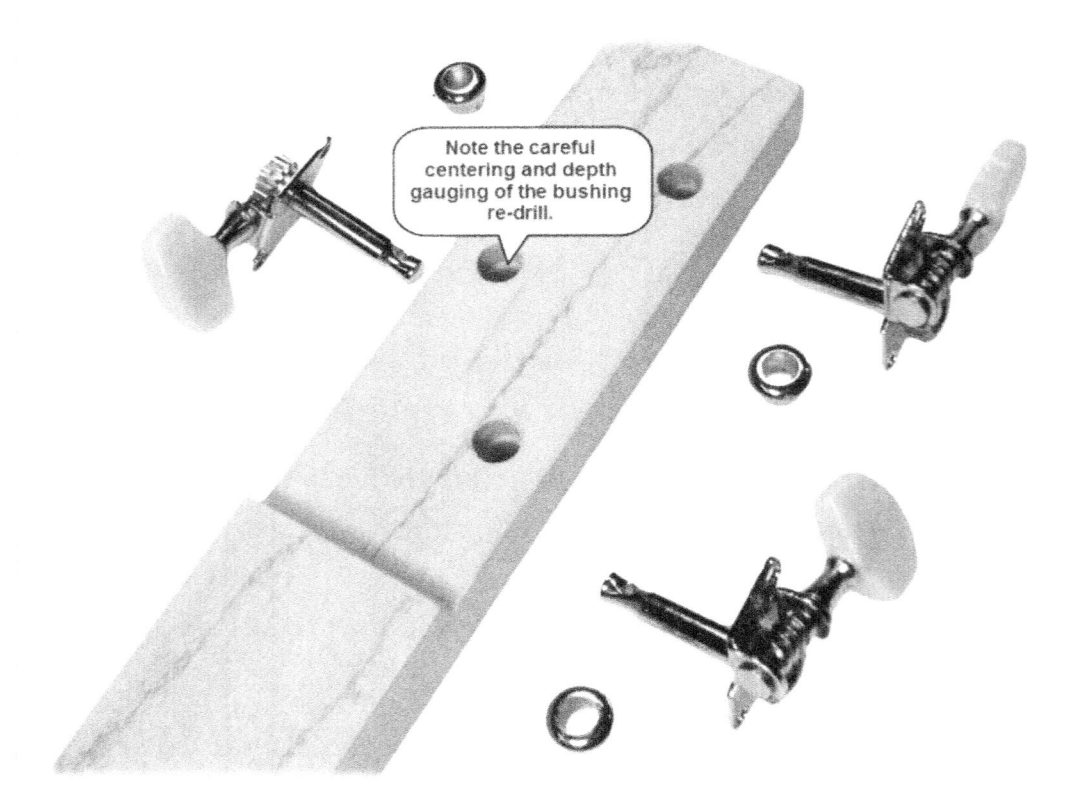

Above: A headstock with tuner holes re-drilled to accommodate the press-in bushing.

Installing the Tuners

Now it is time to insert the tuners (gear towards the body!) and mark the screw mounting holes. You absolutely must pre-drill the screw holes using a 1/16" bit. If you just try to force the delicate screws into the hardwood without pre-drilling, they are almost guaranteed to sheer off.

Make sure that the tuner edges are parallel to the headstock edges, and then mark the center of each hole location with a sharp pencil or fine-point marker.

If at this point you discover that you didn't measure quite right and the tuners are too close together, keep in mind that you can always angle them a bit to get things to fit. Just make sure if you do that the buttons will be able to be fully turned (without hitting the edge of the headstock) and that the mounting plates don't extend past the edge of the headstock.

The tuner gear should be towards the body of the instrument. If it faces towards the top of the headstock, you have the tuner on the wrong side.

***Above:** Dry fitting the tuners and marking the screw holes for pre-drilling.*

Once you've marked the screw locations, remove the tuners and pre-drill the holes with a 1/16" bit, as shown in the photo below.

***PRO TIP:** Use a piece of masking or painter's tape wrapped around your drill bit as a depth guide so you don't accidentally drill all the way through the headstock.*

Above: The back of the headstock with the pre-drilled tuner screw mounting holes.

Finally, tap the bushings into place and then mount the tuners using the screws that came with them. The fully installed tuners should appear similar to those in the photo below. Of course, if you used other tuners your headstock will look different, but the overall layout should generally be the same.

Even though I have stressed how the tuners should be oriented (gears towards the body), if you get to this point and find that something went wrong and one of yours is upside down, it's not the end of the world. A lot of builders, whether accidentally or intentionally, end up mounting their tuners upside down, and usually it works out alright.

The main problem that can arise is that when tuners are mounted upside down, as the string tension increases it can pull the gears apart instead of more tightly together, and this can cause the gears to slip and eventually strip out, rendering the guitar unable to be tuned.

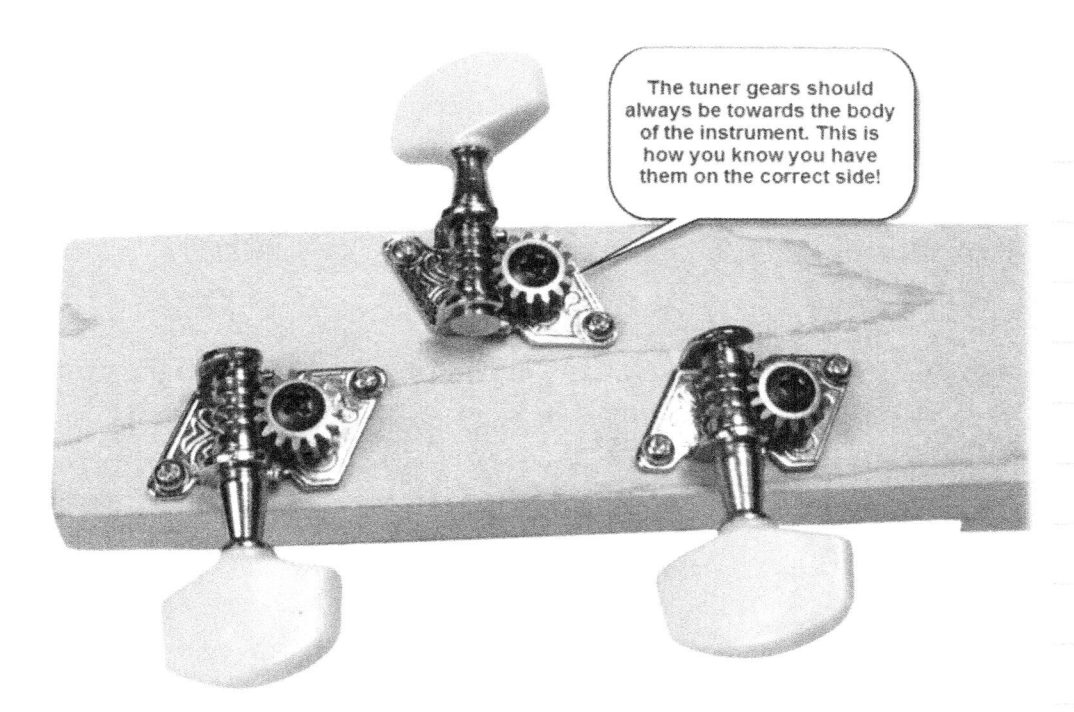

Above: View from the back of the headstock with two left and one right tuner properly installed.

Above: View from the front of the headstock with two left and one right tuner properly installed.

NOTES

(handwritten): ZERO FRET. Maybe a bit higher than rew of frets — gap between 1st fret and strings ideally 0.8mm (0.032")

15. INSTALL THE NUT

As mentioned in the parts sourcing section earlier in this book, there are many different styles of nuts that can be used on a cigar box guitar. For the purposes of this guide, I'll be showing how to use threaded rod nuts, since threaded rods and bolts are usually easily available to most builders.

***PRO TIP:** If using a homemade wooden nut, you will ignore the threaded rod-specific instructions that follow and instead glue your nut to the neck edge of the headstock recess, flush up against the raised part. All measurements later in regard to bridge placement, scale length, etc. will be made from the neck-facing edge of that glued-in-place nut.*

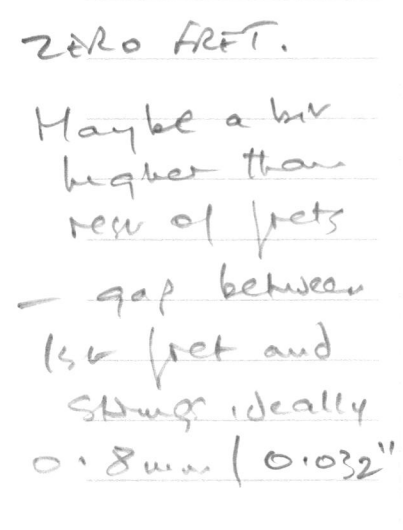

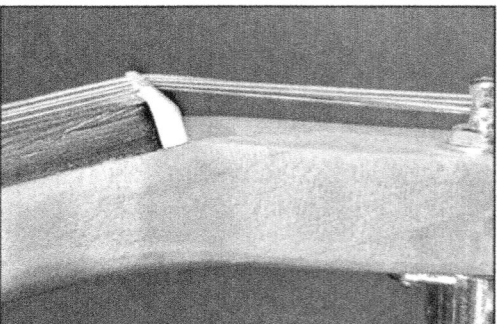

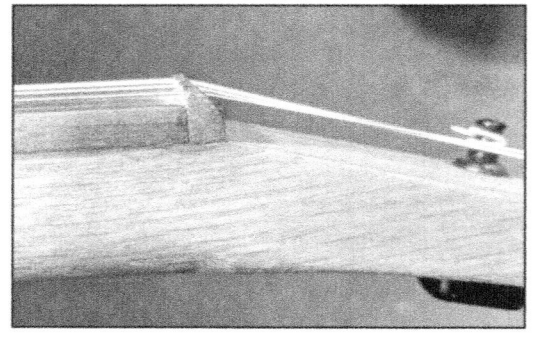

***Above:** As a reminder, here are the photos of some homemade nut examples of the glued-in-place variety. With this style of nut, the scale length is measured from the point where the strings leave the nut headed towards the bridge.*

Proceeding with our threaded rod nut, now it is time to file a groove for it to rest in on the top of the neck, just back from the edge of the headstock recess.

Begin by marking a pair of parallel lines about ¼" from the edge of the headstock tuner cutout, and then use a round file to file a rounded groove into the neck, to end up with what is shown in the photos below. This groove will help keep the nut in place once the guitar is strung up. You can lower the action (height of the strings over the neck) of the instrument by deepening this groove as desired.

If you don't have a round file of the right size, that's OK – a shallow triangular or even square-bottomed slot will work just fine to hold the nut in place.

Above: These two photos show the nut groove filed, and the threaded rod nut resting in the groove. A round file was used to make this groove, but it doesn't have to be rounded at all. A shallow rectangular notch or triangular divot sawed into the wood will work just as well.

16. Install Box Corners (Optional)

If you sourced some box corners, you can now mount them onto the cigar box. For this guide, we'll be showing the installation of the popular brass-plated box corners sold by C. B. Gitty, and included in our basic 3-string CBG kits.

These corners not only look good, but they also help keep the cigar box lid closed. Be sure to start the holes using an awl, or pre-drill the screw holes using an appropriately sized bit. Note that if you have an all-wood cigar box, it may have rounded edges, so it may not be possible to effectively install box corners on it.

Above: A close-up of our cigar box with brass box corners installed.

17. Seal the Box (Optional)

If you are not installing any type of box corners, you will likely need to take steps to seal your cigar box shut. I don't recommend gluing it permanently shut, as you may want to be able to open it back up later.

Your cigar box may already have some sort of clasp or latch on it, and sometimes those are enough. If not, using something like small screws or nails/brads can be a good way to hold it closed. Or if you have a small hinge, you can screw that on as a closure — an actual hasp with a latch works even better. If the side walls of your cigar box aren't thick enough for safely inserting a screw or small nail through the lid, you can always glue/mount a small piece of wood or two inside, just under where the lid comes to rest, and then screw down into that. Or you could screw down through the lid and into the neck over the central part of the box.

18. String It Up

You are now ready to string up your cigar box guitar! We'll be stepping through how to get her tuned to an Open G "GDG" tuning, so hopefully you sourced appropriate strings for that. If you have strings intended for another tuning, go ahead and tune them to that instead – the general steps are the same.

Remember that the largest string (which is tuned to the lowest pitch) goes on the left, if you are looking at the instrument from the front. When holding the guitar in playing position (either right or left-handed), the thickest/lowest-pitched one should be on the top.

Each string is inserted through the appropriate hole in the tailpiece, then run across the cigar box and up the neck, over the nut and then wrapped around the appropriate tuner post.

The photos below show the strings at all key locations on the instrument: strung through the tailpiece hinge, crossing over the bridge, crossing over the nut, and wrapped around the tuner posts. Remember that depending on what strings you sourced, yours may look different: all three may be bronze or nickel-wound, for example.

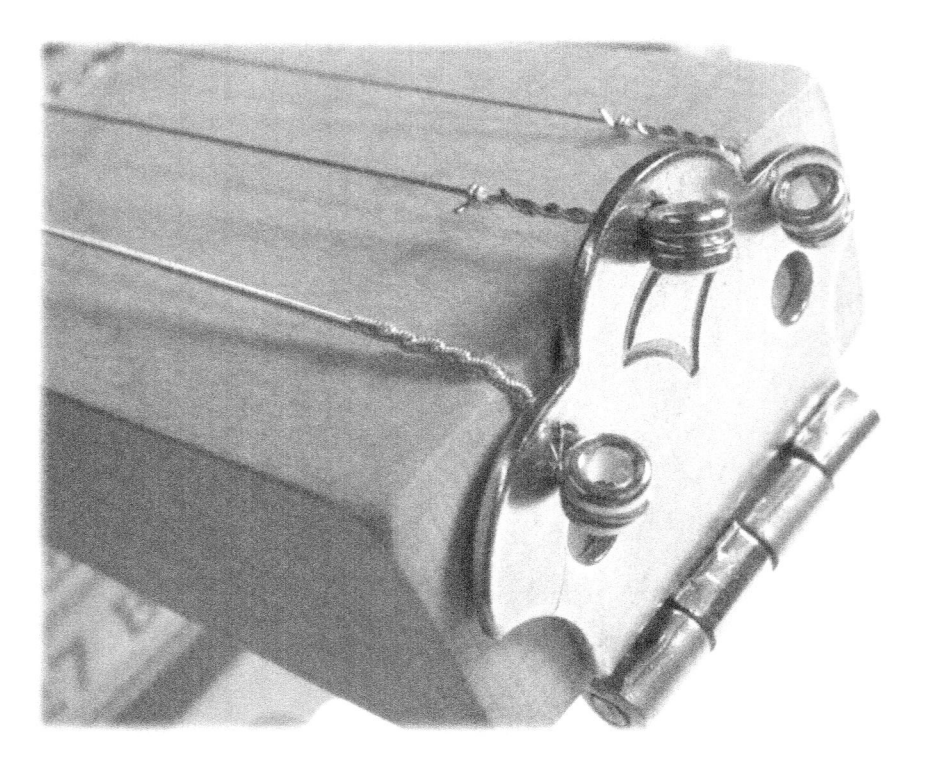

Above: Strings strung through the tailpiece. Depending on the tailpiece method you chose, your guitar may look different.

Above: This photo shows two alternate methods of attaching the strings to a hinge-style tailpiece – up from below, and "noose-style", where the string loops through its own ball end. Note that on this CBG, no neck heel extends through the end of the box, and the tailpiece is screwed right to the side of the box itself. The noose-style can be useful if the holes on your hinge are too big for the ball ends of the strings to not slip through, and you don't want to bother with drilling smaller holes. The "up from below" method only works if the tailpiece is mounted so that it hinges over the surface of the neck/box, and the holes are small enough to keep the string ball from slipping through.

***Above:** The strings run up and over the bridge, and the ridges of the threaded rod help to hold them in the right position, about ½-inch apart. If you prefer a wider or narrower spacing, you are free to adjust as you see fit.*

The threaded rods used for the nut and the bridge help you guide the strings into proper locations with the right spacing between them, with the middle D string centered and the high and low G strings about ½-inch to 5/8-inch on either side of it.

Above: Close-up of the strings running up and over the threaded rod nut. Make sure the nut is resting squarely in its groove before increasing string tension.

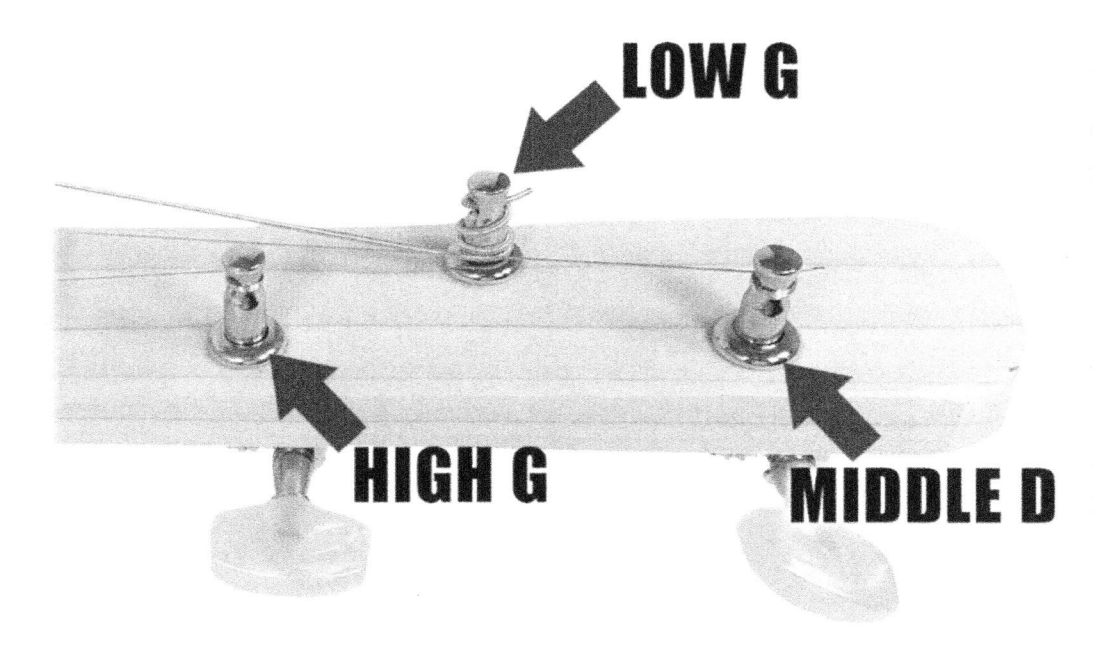

Above: This diagram shows which tuner posts the strings go around. Note that the strings are always wound from the INSIDE edge (from the middle of the headstock).

Wrap each string around its post a couple of times (starting from the inner side) and then insert the end through the hole in the tuner shaft before pulling it taut. Now give the tuner button a few turns, keeping an eye on which way the shaft is rotating to make sure you are tightening it.

Tighten the strings just enough to where they ring out a fairly clean note when plucked without any rattling or excessive looseness. You don't want to get them too tight at this point, and definitely not tight enough to break. You just want a bit of tension on them so you can get the nut and bridge positioned.

Double-check to make sure your nut is laying flat in its groove, and then if you haven't already, lift up all three strings with your finger and slide the bridge into place exactly 25 inches (635mm) from the point where the strings leave the nut. This sets the scale length of your cigar box guitar at

25 inches, which is one of the standard lengths used by many builders.

You can now use your nippers or side cutters to trim the excess length of string sticking out from the tuner posts – leave about ¼" or so of string as shown in the diagram photo above. You should now be ready to proceed to getting the new strings tuned up.

Congratulations!

You built this. This is YOUR cigar box guitar. That is quite an accomplishment, and any music you make on it is guaranteed to mean more to you, to resonate deeper, than if you had just grabbed some factory-made thing off the wall at a chain store. Take a moment to let that sink in!

Above: The author's son Kieran, AKA "Gitty Junior", poses with a three-string CBG he helped his dad build.

Tuning and Playing

Now it's time to get your new cigar box guitar tuned up and get busy making some music.

If you followed my recommendations, you're using strings intended for an open G tuning: on a 3-string CBG the thickest/lowest-pitched string will be "G", the middle string being "D" and the highest string being a higher-pitched "G" (usually one octave above the low G).

It is highly recommended that you utilize a digital chromatic tuner when tuning your cigar box guitar. You can find inexpensive digital chromatic tuners at www.CBGitty.com if you don't already own one. Another handy option are the free apps available for smart phones that turn your phone into a digital tuner.

SLIDE PLAYING

Since this is a fretless guitar, it is meant to be played with a slide. Many things can be used as slides, from wine bottle necks and glass medicine vials to a short lengths of copper pipe, to the edge of an old pocketknife. We also have a wide range of mass-produced and hand-made slides available at CBGitty.com/slides.

Above: Four 2 ¼-inch (~57mm) different guitar slides specifically sized for cigar box guitar playing: brass, copper, stainless steel and glass.

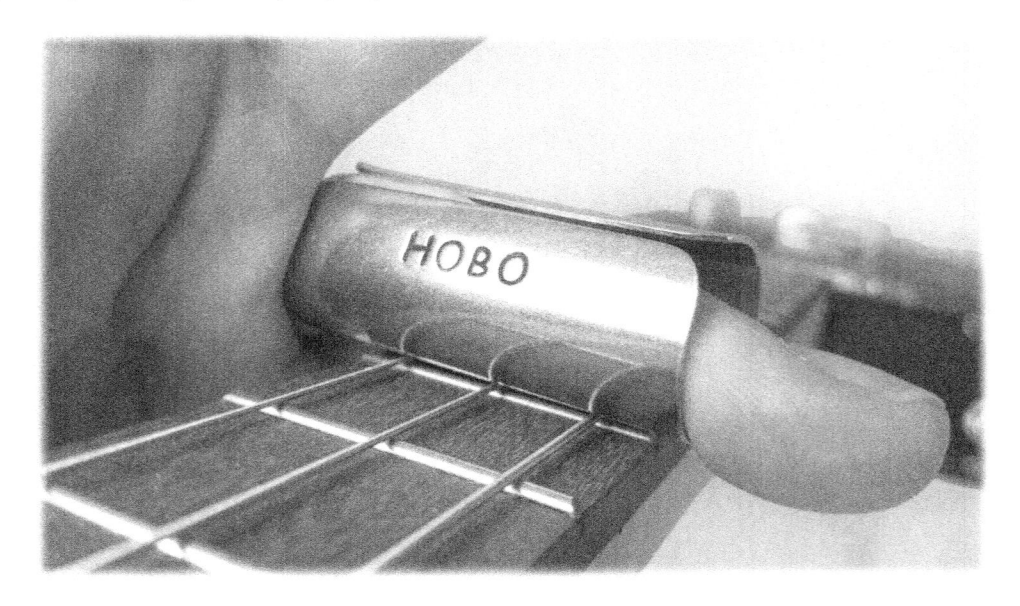

Above: One example of how to wear a slide for CBG playing. In this image, one of C. B. Gitty's adjustable "Hobo" slides, hand-made by master jeweler Ron Hall, is worn on the third/ring finger.

Fret Position Marking

It can be helpful to mark some important fret locations on the neck to make playing easier. The key positions are where the 5th, 7th and 12th frets would be on a fretted neck. Finding these positions can be a bit tricky, but if you have a digital chromatic tuner, and your thinnest string is properly tuned to "G", then move your slide up the string until the tuner registers a "C". That is the 5th fret location, and you can mark this right on the neck.

Now continue moving the slide up until it registers a "D". this is the 7th fret location, which you should mark. Now continue moving the slide up until it registers "G" again. This is the 12th fret location, which marks a full octave from the note of the open string.

For reference, the following diagram shows a rough layout of where fret marks can go, along with where fret position marker dots are usually placed. The chart that follows shows the exact measurements where all frets would be located, if you want to mark all of them or double-check your tuner-based marks. Note that you'll only have room for a certain number of fret marks, depending on the size of your cigar box.

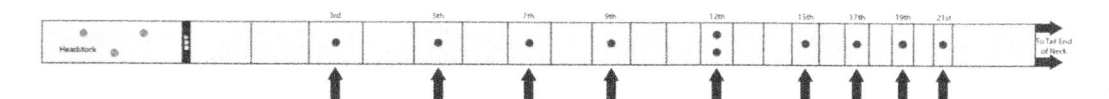

Above: A guide to fret position marker placement.

Fret Position Table for 25-inch Scale Length

Fret #	Distance from Nut (Inches)	Distance from Nut (mm)	Fret Position Marker
1	1.40	35.64	
2	2.73	69.28	
3	3.98	101.03	Yes
4	5.16	131.00	
5	6.27	159.29	Yes
6	7.32	185.99	
7	8.32	211.19	Yes
8	9.25	234.98	
9	10.14	257.43	Yes
10	10.97	278.62	
11	11.76	298.62	
12	12.50	317.50	Yes (Double)
13	13.20	335.32	
14	13.86	352.14	
15	14.49	368.02	Yes
16	15.08	383.00	
17	15.64	397.14	Yes
18	16.16	410.49	
19	16.66	423.09	Yes
20	17.13	434.99	
21	17.57	446.21	Yes

You can find more scale length charts in the appendix at the end of this guide.

Playing Your First Song

With your fret locations marked, you can play some simple 3-chord, 12-bar blues songs by strumming as follows. Each "/" represents one strum, or beat, and each "|" is a separator between 4-beat measures. At the end, simply repeat as many times as you want. Many famous blues songs follow this progression. "Open" means to strum without your slide touching the strings; "fifth" means to place the slide with gentle pressure straight across all three strings, and "seventh" indicates the same thing but up at the seventh fret mark.

Don't try to push the strings all the way down to the neck surface, just use enough pressure to get a clear note when you strum them.

Open　　　　**Fifth**　　　　**Open**　　　　　　　**Fifth**

| / / / / | / / / / | / / / / | / / / / | / / / / | / / / / |

Open　　　　　　　　　**Seventh**　　**Fifth**　　**Open**　　　**Seventh**

| / / / / | / / / / | / / / / | / / / / | / / / / | / / / / |

Playing Your Second Song

This next one is one of the best-known riffs in the blues, used in Muddy Waters' "Hoochie Coochie Man" and many other songs. Listen to the opening of Muddy's classic on YouTube or elsewhere to get the feel of how this is supposed to go. Once you hear it you'll recognize it immediately, but to try to put it into words, the general rhythm is Dunh-DA-dunh-da dunh, dunh, dunh.

Open – Fifth – Open – Third – Open – Open – Open (repeat)

You can find much more information on how to play a CBG at CigarBoxGuitar.com and CigarBoxNation.com. See the Resources section at the end of this guide for links and suggestions.

Troubleshooting

Even with a build this simple, there are plenty of things that can go wrong. Here are some fixes, workarounds and ideas for hiding potential problems.

BUZZING STRINGS

If your strings have a sitar-like buzz when you pluck them, try rotating your nut and bridge a bit. Sometimes a very slight change in how the strings cross the nut and bridge can make the buzzing go away.

Strings are also more likely to buzz if they are too loosely tensioned. If you are deviating from the recommended tuning (GDG), then these may not be the right strings for you.

A nut or bridge that has too wide and flat of a top surface where the strings go across it can also cause buzzing. If your nut or bridge have a wider/flatter top, try filing more of a bevel into one side to narrow it down. This usually isn't an issue with threaded rod nuts/bridges.

BROKEN STRINGS

Strings break if you try to crank them tighter than they were designed to go, and it is common for the beginning builder (and even experienced builders) to break strings. The calculations to try to correctly determine what size strings you should use are pretty complicated, so it is frequently a matter of trial and error. There are free resources over at CigarBoxGuitar.com related to picking the best strings for the tuning you want, be sure to read the articles there for more insight.

You can always buy a replacement string set, or entirely different strings, at CBGitty.com/strings.

Over Cuts, Mis-drilled Holes and Other Problems

Some mistakes are so bad that they are simply unfixable, but usually you can get creative and work around them. Here are some ideas for different key problem areas that you can use to save a build from the wood pile.

Neck slots too big – if you overcut your neck slots, consider making a wooden collar to fit over the neck, which will hide the slot. You can screw this collar right to the box, and it will look like you meant for it to be there all along, especially if you use a nice decorative hard wood.

Drilled a tuner hole in the wrong place – this is a tricky one, but you can always cut a plug to fill the hole, or mount something decorative over top of it, depending on where it is.

Cut the box lid recess too big – If your box lid recess extends out beyond the box, it can be unsightly. But you can get creative and cover it with something decorative – a thin piece of wood cut to shape, a metal embellishment of some sort, etc.

Remember: cigar box guitars are not supposed to be perfect. Don't let minor mistakes ruin your fun - learn from them and try to avoid them when you build your next one!

Closing Thoughts

Fig 10 - The Finished Instrument

Above: An illustration from the original 1880's plans for the "Uncle Enos" cigar box banjo, published by Daniel Carter Beard.

So here you are, after several hours of cutting, drilling and measuring, with a completed cigar box guitar. You have joined the ranks of handmade musical innovators tens of thousands strong, with a legacy dating back thousands of years. Welcome, and congratulations!

I truly hope that the process of building your first cigar box guitar using this guide has been enjoyable and frustration-free. In a project like this where there is such a range of parts and materials that you could be using, it is impossible to cover every possible combination and give detailed instructions for every variation, but I have tried to at least give you enough information for your creative DIY spirit to figure out the rest; and if nothing else, to point you to free resources where you can learn more.

I also hope that you will consider joining the ever-growing online community of people who have "caught the bug" of making their own instruments. CigarBoxNation.com, with over 20,000 members worldwide, is a great place to start. There are also quite a few Facebook groups dedicated to this hobby/obsession, including the "Friends of C. B. Gitty" group, where friendly folks post their photos, ask questions, and share tips and advice.

If you are like many of us, all during this first build you were already thinking about what you'd do differently on your next build. Questions such as "what about a fretted instrument?" or "why not put in an electric guitar pickup?" may have gone through your head. This basic 3-string slide CBG that you have built is just the tip of the iceberg, and you can go on to create ever more amazing things, if you want to. You can even rework this first build to include some fancier additions.

The how-to resources are there for you, many of them free, and inexpensive parts are abundant – many of them designed specifically for use on cigar box guitars. There has literally never been a better time to launch into the amazing hobby of homemade instrument building.

If you choose to go forward with this, always remember these two pieces of advice: that it's always better to Build What You Play, and Play What You Love; and... if you're having fun, you're doing it right!

Ben "Gitty" Baker

November 2019

Appendix 1

Measurement Conversions Chart

Fraction Inch	Decimal Inch	Metric (MM)
1/64	0.01563	0.40
1/32	0.03125	0.79
3/64	0.04688	1.19
1/16	**0.0625**	**1.59**
5/64	0.07813	1.98
3/32	0.09375	2.38
7/64	0.10938	2.78
1/8	**0.125**	**3.18**
9/64	0.14063	3.57
5/32	0.15625	3.97
11/64	0.17188	4.37
3/16	**0.1875**	**4.76**
13/64	0.20313	5.16
7/32	0.21875	5.56
15/64	0.23438	5.95
1/4	**0.25**	**6.35**
17/64	0.26563	6.75
9/32	0.28125	7.14
19/64	0.29688	7.54
5/16	**0.3125**	**7.94**
21/64	0.32813	8.33
11/32	0.34375	8.73
23/64	0.35938	9.13
3/8	**0.375**	**9.53**
25/64	0.39063	9.92
13/32	0.40625	10.32
27/64	0.42188	10.72
7/16	**0.4375**	**11.11**
29/64	0.45313	11.51
15/32	0.46875	11.91
31/64	0.48438	12.30
1/2	**0.5**	**12.70**

Fraction Inch	Decimal Inch	Metric (MM)
33/64	0.51563	13.10
17/32	0.53125	13.49
35/64	0.54688	13.89
9/16	**0.5625**	**14.29**
37/64	0.57813	14.68
19/32	0.59375	15.08
39/64	0.60938	15.48
5/8	**0.625**	**15.88**
41/64	0.64063	16.27
21/32	0.65625	16.67
43/64	0.67188	17.07
11/16	**0.6875**	**17.46**
45/64	0.70313	17.86
23/32	0.71875	18.26
47/64	0.73438	18.65
3/4	**0.75**	**19.05**
49/64	0.76563	19.45
25/32	0.78125	19.84
51/64	0.79688	20.24
13/16	**0.8125**	**20.64**
53/64	0.82813	21.03
27/32	0.84375	21.43
55/64	0.85938	21.83
7/8	**0.875**	**22.23**
57/64	0.89063	22.62
29/32	0.90625	23.02
59/64	0.92188	23.42
15/16	**0.9375**	**23.81**
61/64	0.95313	24.21
31/32	0.96875	24.61
63/64	0.98438	25.00
1	**1**	**25.40**

Appendix 2

Common Scale Length Charts

Use these charts for building cigar box guitars and other instruments to different scales, from short to long. As a general rule, using the metric measurements can help keep your fret positions more accurate even if you don't use metric for anything else. Diatonic fretting, not previously discussed in this guide, is commonly used on dulcimers and canjos.

13-inch Scale
(330.2 mm)
Soprano Ukulele/Violin

Fret #	Inch	MM	Skip for Diatonic
1	0.730	18.5	*
2	1.418	36.0	
3	2.068	52.5	*
4	2.682	68.1	
5	3.261	82.8	
6	3.808	96.7	*
7	4.324	109.8	
8	4.811	122.2	*
9	5.270	133.9	
10	5.704	144.9	
11	6.113	155.3	**
12	**6.500**	**165.1**	
13	6.865	174.4	
14	7.209	183.1	
15	7.534	191.4	*
16	7.841	199.2	
17	8.131	206.5	
18	8.404	213.5	*
19	8.662	220.0	
20	8.905	226.2	*
21	9.135	232.0	
22	9.352	237.5	
23	9.557	242.7	**
24	**9.750**	**247.7**	

13.875-inch Scale
(352.4 mm)
A-style Mandolin

Fret #	Inch	MM	Skip for Diatonic
1	0.779	19.8	*
2	1.514	38.5	
3	2.208	56.1	*
4	2.862	72.7	
5	3.480	88.4	
6	4.064	103.2	*
7	4.615	117.2	
8	5.134	130.4	*
9	5.625	142.9	
10	6.088	154.6	
11	6.525	165.7	**
12	**6.938**	**176.2**	
13	7.327	186.1	
14	7.694	195.4	
15	8.041	204.2	*
16	8.369	212.6	
17	8.678	220.4	
18	8.969	227.8	*
19	9.245	234.8	
20	9.505	241.4	*
21	9.750	247.6	
22	9.981	253.5	
23	10.200	259.1	**
24	**10.406**	**264.3**	

Common Scale Length Charts

14.125-inch Scale
(358.8 mm)
F-style Mandolin

Fret #	Inch	MM	Skip for Diatonic
1	0.793	20.1	*
2	1.541	39.1	
3	2.247	57.1	*
4	2.914	74.0	
5	3.543	90.0	
6	4.137	105.1	*
7	4.698	119.3	
8	5.227	132.8	*
9	5.726	145.4	
10	6.198	157.4	
11	6.643	168.7	**
12	**7.063**	**179.4**	
13	7.459	189.5	
14	7.833	199.0	
15	8.186	207.9	*
16	8.519	216.4	
17	8.834	224.4	
18	9.131	231.9	*
19	9.411	239.0	
20	9.676	245.8	*
21	9.926	252.1	
22	10.161	258.1	
23	10.384	263.7	**
24	**10.594**	**269.1**	

15-inch Scale
(381 mm)
Concert (Alto) Ukulele

Fret #	Inch	MM	Skip for Diatonic
1	0.842	21.4	*
2	1.637	41.6	
3	2.387	60.6	*
4	3.094	78.6	
5	3.763	95.6	
6	4.393	111.6	*
7	4.989	126.7	
8	5.551	141.0	*
9	6.081	154.5	
10	6.582	167.2	
11	7.054	179.2	**
12	**7.500**	**190.5**	
13	7.921	201.2	
14	8.318	211.3	
15	8.693	220.8	*
16	9.047	229.8	
17	9.381	238.3	
18	9.697	246.3	*
19	9.994	253.9	
20	10.275	261.0	*
21	10.540	267.7	
22	10.791	274.1	
23	11.027	280.1	**
24	**11.250**	**285.8**	

Common Scale Length Charts

16-inch Scale
(406.4 mm)

Fret #	Inch	MM	Skip for Diatonic
1	0.898	22.8	*
2	1.746	44.3	
3	2.546	64.7	*
4	3.301	83.8	
5	4.014	101.9	
6	4.686	119.0	*
7	5.321	135.2	
8	5.921	150.4	*
9	6.486	164.8	
10	7.020	178.3	
11	7.524	191.1	**
12	**8.000**	**203.2**	
13	8.449	214.6	
14	8.873	225.4	
15	9.273	235.5	*
16	9.650	245.1	
17	10.007	254.2	
18	10.343	262.7	*
19	10.661	270.8	
20	10.960	278.4	*
21	11.243	285.6	
22	11.510	292.4	
23	11.762	298.8	**
24	**12.000**	**304.8**	

17-inch Scale
(431.8 mm)
Tenor Ukulele

Fret #	Inch	MM	Skip for Diatonic
1	0.954	24.2	*
2	1.855	47.1	
3	2.705	68.7	*
4	3.507	89.1	
5	4.264	108.3	
6	4.979	126.5	*
7	5.654	143.6	
8	6.291	159.8	*
9	6.892	175.1	
10	7.459	189.5	
11	7.995	203.1	**
12	**8.500**	**215.9**	
13	8.977	228.0	
14	9.427	239.5	
15	9.852	250.3	*
16	10.254	260.4	
17	10.632	270.1	
18	10.990	279.1	*
19	11.327	287.7	
20	11.645	295.8	*
21	11.946	303.4	
22	12.230	310.6	
23	12.497	317.4	**
24	**12.750**	**323.9**	

Common Scale Length Charts

18-inch Scale
(457.2 mm)

Fret #	Inch	MM	Skip for Diatonic
1	1.010	25.7	*
2	1.964	49.9	
3	2.864	72.7	*
4	3.713	94.3	
5	4.515	114.7	
6	5.272	133.9	*
7	5.986	152.1	
8	6.661	169.2	*
9	7.297	185.3	
10	7.898	200.6	
11	8.465	215.0	**
12	**9.000**	**228.6**	
13	9.505	241.4	
14	9.982	253.5	
15	10.432	265.0	*
16	10.857	275.8	
17	11.258	285.9	
18	11.636	295.6	*
19	11.993	304.6	
20	12.330	313.2	*
21	12.649	321.3	
22	12.949	328.9	
23	13.232	336.1	**
24	**13.500**	**342.9**	

19-inch Scale
(482.6 mm)
Baritone Ukulele

Fret #	Inch	MM	Skip for Diatonic
1	1.066	27.1	*
2	2.073	52.7	
3	3.023	76.8	*
4	3.920	99.6	
5	4.766	121.1	
6	5.565	141.4	*
7	6.319	160.5	
8	7.031	178.6	*
9	7.703	195.6	
10	8.337	211.7	
11	8.935	227.0	**
12	**9.500**	**241.3**	
13	10.033	254.8	
14	10.536	267.6	
15	11.011	279.7	*
16	11.460	291.1	
17	11.883	301.8	
18	12.282	312.0	*
19	12.660	321.6	
20	13.015	330.6	*
21	13.351	339.1	
22	13.668	347.2	
23	13.968	354.8	**
24	**14.250**	**362.0**	

Common Scale Length Charts

20-inch Scale
(508 mm)

Fret #	Inch	MM	Skip for Diatonic
1	1.123	28.5	*
2	2.182	55.4	
3	3.182	80.8	*
4	4.126	104.8	
5	5.017	127.4	
6	5.858	148.8	*
7	6.652	169.0	
8	7.401	188.0	*
9	8.108	205.9	
10	8.775	222.9	
11	9.405	238.9	**
12	**10.000**	**254.0**	
13	10.561	268.3	
14	11.091	281.7	
15	11.591	294.4	*
16	12.063	306.4	
17	12.508	317.7	
18	12.929	328.4	*
19	13.326	338.5	
20	13.700	348.0	*
21	14.054	357.0	
22	14.388	365.4	
23	14.703	373.4	**
24	**15.000**	**381.0**	

21-inch Scale
(533.4 mm)

Short Irish Tenor Banjo

Fret #	Inch	MM	Skip for Diatonic
1	1.179	29.9	*
2	2.291	58.2	
3	3.341	84.9	*
4	4.332	110.0	
5	5.268	133.8	
6	6.151	156.2	*
7	6.984	177.4	
8	7.771	197.4	*
9	8.513	216.2	
10	9.214	234.0	
11	9.876	250.8	**
12	**10.500**	**266.7**	
13	11.089	281.7	
14	11.646	295.8	
15	12.171	309.1	*
16	12.666	321.7	
17	13.134	333.6	
18	13.575	344.8	*
19	13.992	355.4	
20	14.385	365.4	*
21	14.757	374.8	
22	15.107	383.7	
23	15.438	392.1	**
24	**15.750**	**400.1**	

Common Scale Length Charts

22-inch Scale
(558.8 mm)

Fret #	Inch	MM	Skip for Diatonic
1	1.235	31.4	*
2	2.400	61.0	
3	3.500	88.9	*
4	4.539	115.3	
5	5.519	140.2	
6	6.444	163.7	*
7	7.317	185.8	
8	8.141	206.8	*
9	8.919	226.5	
10	9.653	245.2	
11	10.346	262.8	**
12	**11.000**	**279.4**	
13	11.617	295.1	
14	12.200	309.9	
15	12.750	323.9	*
16	13.269	337.0	
17	13.759	349.5	
18	14.222	361.2	*
19	14.658	372.3	
20	15.070	382.8	*
21	15.459	392.7	
22	15.826	402.0	
23	16.173	410.8	**
24	**16.500**	**419.1**	

22.25-inch Scale
(565.2 mm)
Tenor Banjo

Fret #	Inch	MM	Skip for Diatonic
1	1.249	31.7	*
2	2.428	61.7	
3	3.540	89.9	*
4	4.590	116.6	
5	5.581	141.8	
6	6.517	165.5	*
7	7.400	188.0	
8	8.233	209.1	*
9	9.020	229.1	
10	9.763	248.0	
11	10.463	265.8	**
12	**11.125**	**282.6**	
13	11.749	298.4	
14	12.339	313.4	
15	12.895	327.5	*
16	13.420	340.9	
17	13.916	353.5	
18	14.383	365.3	*
19	14.825	376.6	
20	15.242	387.1	*
21	15.635	397.1	
22	16.006	406.6	
23	16.357	415.5	**
24	**16.688**	**423.9**	

Common Scale Length Charts

23-inch Scale
(584.2 mm)
Tenor Guitar

Fret #	Inch	MM	Skip for Diatonic
1	1.291	32.8	*
2	2.509	63.7	
3	3.659	92.9	*
4	4.745	120.5	
5	5.769	146.5	
6	6.737	171.1	*
7	7.649	194.3	
8	8.511	216.2	*
9	9.324	236.8	
10	10.092	256.3	
11	10.816	274.7	**
12	**11.500**	**292.1**	
13	12.145	308.5	
14	12.755	324.0	
15	13.330	338.6	*
16	13.872	352.4	
17	14.385	365.4	
18	14.868	377.7	*
19	15.325	389.2	
20	15.755	400.2	*
21	16.162	410.5	
22	16.546	420.3	
23	16.908	429.5	**
24	**17.250**	**438.2**	

23.5-inch Scale
(596.9 mm)

Fret #	Inch	MM	Skip for Diatonic
1	1.319	33.5	*
2	2.564	65.1	
3	3.739	95.0	*
4	4.848	123.1	
5	5.895	149.7	
6	6.883	174.8	*
7	7.816	198.5	
8	8.696	220.9	*
9	9.527	242.0	
10	10.311	261.9	
11	11.051	280.7	**
12	**11.750**	**298.5**	
13	12.409	315.2	
14	13.032	331.0	
15	13.619	345.9	*
16	14.174	360.0	
17	14.697	373.3	
18	15.191	385.9	*
19	15.658	397.7	
20	16.098	408.9	*
21	16.513	419.4	
22	16.906	429.4	
23	17.276	438.8	**
24	**17.625**	**447.7**	

Common Scale Length Charts

24-inch Scale
(609.6 mm)

Fret #	Inch	MM	Skip for Diatonic
1	1.347	34.2	*
2	2.618	66.5	
3	3.818	97.0	*
4	4.951	125.8	
5	6.020	152.9	
6	7.029	178.5	*
7	7.982	202.7	
8	8.881	225.6	*
9	9.730	247.1	
10	10.530	267.5	
11	11.286	286.7	**
12	**12.000**	**304.8**	
13	12.674	321.9	
14	13.309	338.1	
15	13.909	353.3	*
16	14.476	367.7	
17	15.010	381.3	
18	15.515	394.1	*
19	15.991	406.2	
20	16.440	417.6	*
21	16.865	428.4	
22	17.265	438.5	
23	17.643	448.1	**
24	**18.000**	**457.2**	

24.5-inch Scale
(622.3 mm)
Short-Scale Guitar

Fret #	Inch	MM	Skip for Diatonic
1	1.375	34.9	*
2	2.673	67.9	
3	3.898	99.0	*
4	5.054	128.4	
5	6.146	156.1	
6	7.176	182.3	*
7	8.148	207.0	
8	9.066	230.3	*
9	9.932	252.3	
10	10.750	273.0	
11	11.522	292.6	**
12	**12.250**	**311.2**	
13	12.938	328.6	
14	13.586	345.1	
15	14.199	360.7	*
16	14.777	375.3	
17	15.323	389.2	
18	15.838	402.3	*
19	16.324	414.6	
20	16.783	426.3	*
21	17.216	437.3	
22	17.625	447.7	
23	18.011	457.5	**
24	**18.375**	**466.7**	

Common Scale Length Charts

24.75-inch Scale
(628.7 mm)
Gibson & Guild Guitars

Fret #	Inch	MM	Skip for Diatonic
1	1.389	35.3	*
2	2.700	68.6	
3	3.938	100.0	*
4	5.106	129.7	
5	6.208	157.7	
6	7.249	184.1	*
7	8.231	209.1	
8	9.158	232.6	*
9	10.034	254.9	
10	10.860	275.8	
11	11.639	295.6	**
12	**12.375**	**314.3**	
13	13.070	332.0	
14	13.725	348.6	
15	14.344	364.3	*
16	14.928	379.2	
17	15.479	393.2	
18	16.000	406.4	*
19	16.491	418.9	
20	16.954	430.6	*
21	17.392	441.8	
22	17.805	452.2	
23	18.195	462.1	**
24	**18.563**	**471.5**	

25-inch Scale
(635 mm)
Paul Reed Smith, National

Fret #	Inch	MM	Skip for Diatonic
1	1.403	35.6	*
2	2.728	69.3	
3	3.978	101.0	*
4	5.157	131.0	
5	6.271	159.3	
6	7.322	186.0	*
7	8.315	211.2	
8	9.251	235.0	*
9	10.135	257.4	
10	10.969	278.6	
11	11.757	298.6	**
12	**12.500**	**317.5**	
13	13.202	335.3	
14	13.864	352.1	
15	14.489	368.0	*
16	15.079	383.0	
17	15.636	397.1	
18	16.161	410.5	*
19	16.657	423.1	
20	17.125	435.0	*
21	17.567	446.2	
22	17.985	456.8	
23	18.378	466.8	**
24	**18.750**	**476.3**	

Common Scale Length Charts

25.5-inch Scale
(647.7 mm)
Fender Tele & Strat

Fret #	Inch	MM	Skip for Diatonic
1	1.431	36.4	*
2	2.782	70.7	
3	4.057	103.1	*
4	5.261	133.6	
5	6.397	162.5	
6	7.469	189.7	*
7	8.481	215.4	
8	9.436	239.7	*
9	10.338	262.6	
10	11.189	284.2	
11	11.992	304.6	**
12	**12.750**	**323.9**	
13	13.466	342.0	
14	14.141	359.2	
15	14.779	375.4	*
16	15.380	390.7	
17	15.948	405.1	
18	16.484	418.7	*
19	16.990	431.6	
20	17.468	443.7	*
21	17.919	455.1	
22	18.344	465.9	
23	18.746	476.1	**
24	**19.125**	**485.8**	

26-inch Scale
(660.4 mm)

Fret #	Inch	MM	Skip for Diatonic
1	1.459	37.1	*
2	2.837	72.1	
3	4.137	105.1	*
4	5.364	136.2	
5	6.522	165.7	
6	7.615	193.4	*
7	8.647	219.6	
8	9.621	244.4	*
9	10.540	267.7	
10	11.408	289.8	
11	12.227	310.6	**
12	**13.000**	**330.2**	
13	13.730	348.7	
14	14.418	366.2	
15	15.068	382.7	*
16	15.682	398.3	
17	16.261	413.0	
18	16.808	426.9	*
19	17.324	440.0	
20	17.811	452.4	*
21	18.270	464.1	
22	18.704	475.1	
23	19.113	485.5	**
24	**19.500**	**495.3**	

Common Scale Length Charts

26.25-inch Scale
(666.8 mm)
Gibson Banjo

Fret #	Inch	MM	Skip for Diatonic
1	1.473	37.4	*
2	2.864	72.7	
3	4.176	106.1	*
4	5.415	137.6	
5	6.585	167.3	
6	7.688	195.3	*
7	8.730	221.7	
8	9.714	246.7	*
9	10.642	270.3	
10	11.518	292.5	
11	12.345	313.6	**
12	**13.125**	**333.4**	
13	13.862	352.1	
14	14.557	369.7	
15	15.213	386.4	*
16	15.833	402.2	
17	16.417	417.0	
18	16.969	431.0	*
19	17.490	444.2	
20	17.982	456.7	*
21	18.446	468.5	
22	18.884	479.6	
23	19.297	490.2	**
24	**19.688**	**500.1**	

27-inch Scale
(685.8 mm)

Fret #	Inch	MM	Skip for Diatonic
1	1.515	38.5	*
2	2.946	74.8	
3	4.296	109.1	*
4	5.570	141.5	
5	6.773	172.0	
6	7.908	200.9	*
7	8.980	228.1	
8	9.991	253.8	*
9	10.946	278.0	
10	11.847	300.9	
11	12.697	322.5	**
12	**13.500**	**342.9**	
13	14.258	362.1	
14	14.973	380.3	
15	15.648	397.5	*
16	16.285	413.6	
17	16.886	428.9	
18	17.454	443.3	*
19	17.990	456.9	
20	18.496	469.8	*
21	18.973	481.9	
22	19.423	493.4	
23	19.849	504.2	**
24	**20.250**	**514.4**	

Common Scale Length Charts

27.5-inch Scale
(698.5 mm)
Baritone Guitar

Fret #	Inch	MM	Skip for Diatonic
1	1.543	39.2	*
2	3.000	76.2	
3	4.375	111.1	*
4	5.673	144.1	
5	6.898	175.2	
6	8.055	204.6	*
7	9.146	232.3	
8	10.176	258.5	*
9	11.148	283.2	
10	12.066	306.5	
11	12.932	328.5	**
12	**13.750**	**349.3**	
13	14.522	368.9	
14	15.250	387.4	
15	15.938	404.8	*
16	16.587	421.3	
17	17.199	436.9	
18	17.777	451.5	*
19	18.323	465.4	
20	18.838	478.5	*
21	19.324	490.8	
22	19.783	502.5	
23	20.216	513.5	**
24	**20.625**	**523.9**	

28-inch Scale
(711.2 mm)
*Appalachian Dulcimer**

Fret #	Inch	MM	Skip for Diatonic
1	1.572	39.9	*
2	3.055	77.6	
3	4.455	113.2	*
4	5.776	146.7	
5	7.024	178.4	
6	8.201	208.3	*
7	9.312	236.5	
8	10.361	263.2	*
9	11.351	288.3	
10	12.286	312.1	
11	13.168	334.5	**
12	**14.000**	**355.6**	
13	14.786	375.6	
14	15.527	394.4	
15	16.227	412.2	*
16	16.888	429.0	
17	17.512	444.8	
18	18.101	459.8	*
19	18.656	473.9	
20	19.181	487.2	*
21	19.676	499.8	
22	20.143	511.6	
23	20.584	522.8	**
24	**21.000**	**533.4**	

* Appalachian dulcimers vary widely in scale, from 25 inches up to 30+ inches. This is just one possible scale to use.

Common Scale Length Charts

29-inch Scale
(736.6 mm)

Fret #	Inch	MM	Skip for Diatonic
1	1.628	41.3	*
2	3.164	80.4	
3	4.614	117.2	*
4	5.983	152.0	
5	7.275	184.8	
6	8.494	215.7	*
7	9.645	245.0	
8	10.731	272.6	*
9	11.756	298.6	
10	12.724	323.2	
11	13.638	346.4	**
12	**14.500**	**368.3**	
13	15.314	389.0	
14	16.082	408.5	
15	16.807	426.9	*
16	17.491	444.3	
17	18.137	460.7	
18	18.747	476.2	*
19	19.322	490.8	
20	19.866	504.6	*
21	20.378	517.6	
22	20.862	529.9	
23	21.319	541.5	**
24	**21.750**	**552.5**	

30-inch Scale
(762 mm)
Short-scale Fender Bass

Fret #	Inch	MM	Skip for Diatonic
1	1.684	42.8	*
2	3.273	83.1	
3	4.773	121.2	*
4	6.189	157.2	
5	7.525	191.1	
6	8.787	223.2	*
7	9.977	253.4	
8	11.101	282.0	*
9	12.162	308.9	
10	13.163	334.3	
11	14.108	358.3	**
12	**15.000**	**381.0**	
13	15.842	402.4	
14	16.637	422.6	
15	17.387	441.6	*
16	18.094	459.6	
17	18.763	476.6	
18	19.393	492.6	*
19	19.989	507.7	
20	20.551	522.0	*
21	21.081	535.5	
22	21.582	548.2	
23	22.054	560.2	**
24	**22.500**	**571.5**	

Common Scale Length Charts

32.25-inch Scale
(736.6 mm)
Long-Neck Banjo

Fret #	Inch	MM	Skip for Diatonic
1	1.628	41.3	*
2	3.164	80.4	
3	4.614	117.2	*
4	5.983	152.0	
5	7.275	184.8	
6	8.494	215.7	*
7	9.645	245.0	
8	10.731	272.6	*
9	11.756	298.6	
10	12.724	323.2	
11	13.638	346.4	**
12	**14.500**	**368.3**	
13	15.314	389.0	
14	16.082	408.5	
15	16.807	426.9	*
16	17.491	444.3	
17	18.137	460.7	
18	18.747	476.2	*
19	19.322	490.8	
20	19.866	504.6	*
21	20.378	517.6	
22	20.862	529.9	
23	21.319	541.5	**
24	**21.750**	**552.5**	

34-inch Scale
(863.6 mm)
Long-scale Electric Bass

Fret #	Inch	MM	Skip for Diatonic
1	1.908	48.5	*
2	3.709	94.2	
3	5.410	137.4	*
4	7.014	178.2	
5	8.529	216.6	
6	9.958	252.9	*
7	11.308	287.2	
8	12.581	319.6	*
9	13.783	350.1	
10	14.918	378.9	
11	15.989	406.1	**
12	**17.000**	**431.8**	
13	17.954	456.0	
14	18.855	478.9	
15	19.705	500.5	*
16	20.507	520.9	
17	21.264	540.1	
18	21.979	558.3	*
19	22.654	575.4	
20	23.291	591.6	*
21	23.892	606.9	
22	24.459	621.3	
23	24.995	634.9	**
24	**25.500**	**647.7**	

References & Resources

There are a number of references you can use to learn more about cigar box guitars, and homemade instrument building in general.

CBGitty.com – As the premiere supplier of parts, kits and gear to the cigar box guitar and homemade music movement, C. B. Gitty is your go-to source for all of the tools and parts you need for your building endeavors. See the Buyer's Guide at the end of this book for help in finding specific cigar box guitar parts available from C. B. Gitty.

If you prefer more of a guided approach to homemade instrument building, be sure to check out the line of innovative kits from C. B. Gitty. We have been working hard over the past few years to create a range of awesome, easy-to-build kits that can get you started on your homemade musical journey.

See the full line here: **https://CBGitty.com/Kits**

CigarBoxNation.com - Cigar Box Nation is the home base and nerve center of the worldwide homemade/handmade instruments movement. In addition to information about cigar box guitars, you can find a vast collection of photos, videos, forum posts and more related to CBGs, canjos, washtub basses and all sorts of other handmade instruments.

There is a wealth of how-to knowledge and advice here, posted by builders like you over the past decade, and if you can't find the answer you can always post your question in one of the forums.

Cigar Box Nation also maintains a Facebook page at https://Facebook.com/CigarBoxNation, with regular posts and features about cigar box guitars and other homemade instruments.

CigarBoxGuitar.com – This is the free knowledgebase library for the homemade music movement. The site is full of articles with how-to-build and how-to-play information, as well as a repository of free homemade instrument plans, photos of celebrities playing cigar box guitars, historic photos of homemade instruments, and much more.

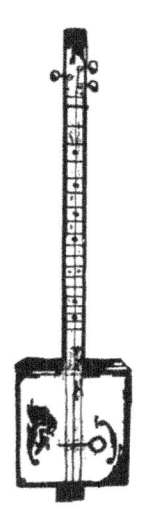

There is also a growing library of free canjo and cigar box guitar tablature available on this site. Just click the "Canjo Tablature" or "Cigar Box Guitar Tablature" link in the right-hand menu to access it.

Selections include some more modern songs, with pieces by The Beatles, the Violent Femmes, Bob Dylan, Elvis, Willy Nelson, Johnny Cash and more, in addition to traditional public domain songs. There are also resources and video links on how to build and play the cigar box guitars - all for free!

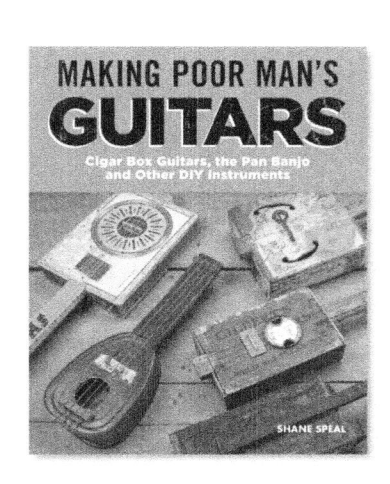

"Making Poor Man's Guitars" Book by Shane Speal – This book, available from C. B. Gitty (https://CBGitty.com/SpealBook) is the definitive printed work on homemade instruments and their history. Shane has been living, eating and breathing cigar box guitars and other homemade instruments for over 25 years, researching their history, building them, performing on them, studying the people who played them, and sharing information with others.

This book represents the encapsulation of his life work. It is part how-to guide, as he walks you through building interesting homemade instruments; it is part religious tract, as he preaches the gospel of the cigar box guitar; it is part history lesson, as he shares interesting stories and facts from his vast knowledge of DIY music history; and it is part motivational seminar, inspiring people to get out there and build instruments and make music on them.

If you are building homemade instruments, you need this book. If you are thinking about building homemade instruments, you need this book. There are other good books on the subject out there, but this one stands alone.

OTHER RECOMMENDED BOOKS

Handmade Music Factory

By Mike Orr

https://CBGitty.com/OrrBook

This was the first of the books to be published following the revival of the modern homemade instrument movement. Mike Orr has been building and playing cigar box guitars and other homemade instruments for years, and in this book he walks you through how to create a number of awesome builds.

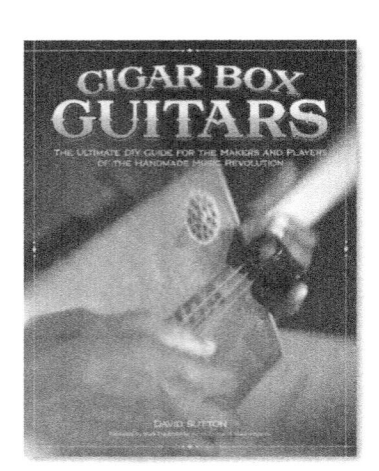

Cigar Box Guitars

By David Sutton

https://CBGitty.com/SuttonBook

This book is part how-to manual and part photographic art, as its artist David Sutton is a professional photographer in addition to being a cigar box guitar enthusiast. David showcases the creations of a number of builders who were prominent at the time of the book's writing, including Shane Speal, the King of the Cigar Box Guitar. He also provides some solid how-to material.

The Folk Art Instrument Builder's Guide

By Charles Atchison

https://CBGitty.com/AtchisonBook

This self-published book by instrument builder and folk instrument historian/collector Charles Atchison is a great reference for the construction of functional folk art & roots instruments, containing 200 pages with over 400 pictures and illustrations and clear instructions for each topic.

This book provides detailed instructions for building the following instruments: One String Diddley Bow, Relic style 4 string Cigar Box Guitar, Tenor Hubcap Banjo, Cajon Drum, Kalimba/Thumb piano, and Washtub Bass (Gutbucket).

It also includes instructions for making your own wooden peg tuners, making your own electric pickups, wiring the instrument, scarf-jointing necks, how to give your instruments that distressed "reliced" look and much, much more.

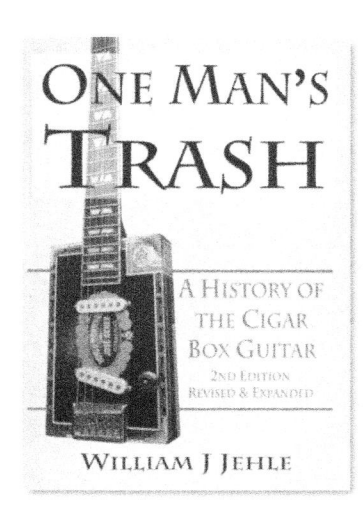

One Man's Trash: A History of the Cigar Box Guitar

2nd Edition

By William Jehle

https://amzn.to/2FOYbCi

This is the definitive history of cigar box fiddles, banjos and guitars, presenting many original sources. A fascinating read for students of musical instrument and DIY history.

Educational Outreach

We have worked with many teachers all around the United States and internationally to help them get instrument building projects added to their school's curriculum. Building handmade instruments fits nicely into most STEAM (Science, Technology, Engineering, Arts & Math) programs!

We have created a number of kits and packages specifically for teachers, from basic one-string canjos (tin can banjos) through more advanced electric guitars. Teachers from grades 3 through 12 have used our kits and parts to teach everything from art and basic music theory and performance through advanced placement high school science courses studying the physics of electrical waves and sound.

If you know of a school or teacher that might be interested in this idea, let them know about us! We also work with summer camps, church groups, Boy Scout troops, community centers, senior centers, and folks wanting to host a local workshop.

E-mail us at **cbgitty@cbgitty.com** to get the ball rolling!

Buyer's Guide

TOOLS

Name	Cost	Brand	Shopping Link	Description
Digital Calipers	$$	Various	https://amzn.to/2HZfFyb	A useful tool to have on the bench both for fretting and general instrument building
Ruler	$	Various	https://amzn.to/2WPwdvY	An 18-inch or 24-inch stainless steel ruler with both imperial and metric markings is a must-have for any fretter.
Fretting Scale Templates	$-$$	C. B. Gitty	https://CBGitty.com/FretTemplate	The best way to get perfect fret layouts without having to measure with a ruler.
Deluxe Fretting Saw	$$	C. B. Gitty	https://CBGitty.com/FretSaw	A must-have for cutting perfect fret slots.
Basic Miter Box	$	C. B. Gitty	https://CBGitty.com/BasicMiterKit	A basic solution for cutting straight fret slots in cigar box guitar necks and fretboards.
Deluxe Miter Box	$$	C. B. Gitty	https://CBGitty.com/DeluxeMiterKit	A sturdy and elegant miter box for cutting perfect fret slots in cigar box guitar necks and fretboards.
Fretting Hammer	$$	C. B. Gitty	https://CBGitty.com/FretHammer	A durable 12-ounce brass head dead blow-style hammer perfect for fretwork and other light hammering tasks. Used in the C. B. Gitty shop.
End Nippers/Fret Cutters	$$	C. B. Gitty	https://CBGitty.com/FretNippers	Specially ground end nippers that cut fret ends nice and flush with the edge of the fretboard. Reduces the amount of filing to be done after cutting.
Fine-tooth Flat File	$	Various	https://amzn.to/2HPMGNa	A good basic file for fret end filing, beveling and leveling.
Diamond Flat File	$$	Various	https://amzn.to/2WOWdHM	Diamond files are more durable than standard files and are great for fine fret work.
Needle File Set	$$	Various	https://amzn.to/2WJ1y34	A basic set of needle files that includes a triangular-profile file that can be converted into a DIY fret end dressing tool.

Buyer's Guide (continued)

Name	Cost	Brand	Shopping Link	Description
Fret End Dressing File	$$$	Stewart-MacDonald	https://amzn.to/2HNc9GZ	A special file designed specifically for fret end dressing. We have been using these in the C. B. Gitty shop for years.
Blue Painter's Tape	$	Scotch	https://amzn.to/2I2WdQR	Great for all sorts of uses, including fretboard protection, depth stop marking, etc.
Fine-grit Sandpaper Pack	$	Various	https://amzn.to/2FLJ5vS	Fine-grit sandpaper is good for doing final smoothing and polishing of dressed fret ends.
"0000" Fine Steel Wool	$	Various	https://amzn.to/2UjlSvl	Great for polishing frets back to a mirror shine.
Superglue	$	Various	https://amzn.to/2I24Vig	Always a handy thing to have around when fretting.

PARTS

Name	Cost	Brand	Shopping Link	Description
Open-Gear Tuners	$	C. B. Gitty	https://CBGitty.com/EconoTuners	The most popular set of inexpensive open-gear tuners for cigar box guitar building. This 6-pack will let you build two 3-string CBGs.
Medium/Medium Nickel-Silver Fret Wire	$	C. B. Gitty	https://CBGitty.com/MediumMedium	The most-used profile for cigar box guitars, conventional guitars and other guitar-scale instruments. Used extensively at C. B. Gitty for most of our pre-made necks and fretboards.
Jumbo Nickel-Silver Fret Wire	$	C. B. Gitty	https://CBGitty.com/Jumbo	One of the largest fret wire profiles, good for basses, specialty electric guitars and also for use as zero frets.

Buyer's Guide (continued)

Tailpieces	$	C. B. Gitty	https://CBGitty.com/Tailpieces	A collection of tailpieces designed specifically for cigar box guitars,.
Nuts and Bridges	$	C. B. Gitty	https://CBGitty.com/Nuts&Bridges	A large selection of nuts and bridges for use on CBGs, many of them designed and manufactured by C. B. Gitty.
Sound Hole Covers & Inserts	$	C. B. Gitty	https://CBGitty.com/SoundHoleCovers	Dress up your next build with a decorative sound hole cover or insert.
Other Parts & Hardware	$-$$	C. B. Gitty	https://CBGitty.com/CBGParts	A collection of some of the best and most popular general parts and hardware for cigar box guitars: tuners, necks, fretboards, pickups, electronics and more.

DIY Musical Instrument Kits

by C. B. Gitty

$79.99

PURE & SIMPLE CIGAR BOX GUITAR KIT - UNFRETTED
Our flagship UNFRETTED (SLIDE) cigar box guitar kit. Includes everything you need, and only requires a screwdriver to assemble. Goes together in under an hour, and sounds great.. Ages 14+.

$99.99

PURE & SIMPLE CIGAR BOX GUITAR KIT - FRETTED
Our flagship FRETTED cigar box guitar kit. Includes everything you need, and only requires a screwdriver to assemble. Goes together in under an hour, and sounds great! Ages 14+.

$79.99

CIGAR BOX UKULELE KIT
Build a classic cigar box ukulele... just like the ones the Hawaiian masters experimented with 100+ years ago, when designing the first ukuleles! Ages 16+.

$59.99

GITTYLELE DIY UKULELE KIT
These ukuleles have a distinctive design and a great sound... and they are fun and easy to build! Ages 14+.

$24.99

CIGAR BOX DIDDLEY BOW KIT
Diddley bows helped create the Blues! Inspired by classic instruments from the Mississippi Delta, this is one of our easiest kits. Ages 14+.

$29.99

AMERICAN CANJO KIT
What's more fun than a simple one-string tin can banjo. Perfect for both young and young-at-heart pickers. Ages 12+.

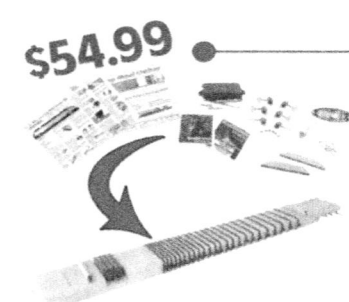

$54.99

2X4 LAP STEEL GUITAR KIT
You supply the 2x4, we supply the parts and how-to! Yields a six-string lap steel slide guitar, perfect for country & western or Hawaiian-style playing. Ages 14+.

$49.99

CIGAR BOX AMPLIFIER KIT
Create a rocking amplifier to go with your cigar box guitar or electric guitar! Some soldering required. Ages 14+.

$19.99

TIN CAN MICROPHONE KIT
Build a mic that captures that vintage AM radio sound! No soldering required. Ages 14+

Order Now! www.CBGitty.com/Kits

3-String Guitar Songbooks

Make even more great music on your new Cigar Box Guitar!

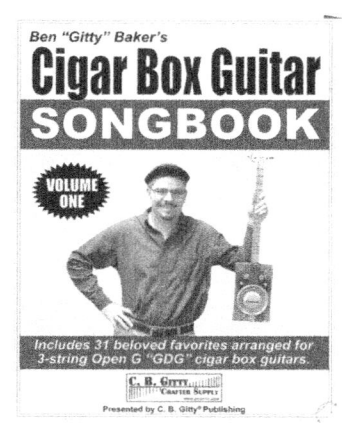

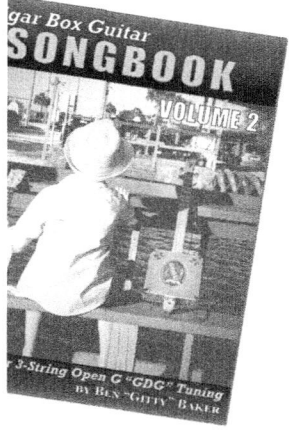

3-STRING CIGAR BOX GUITAR SONGBOOKS, Volumes 1 - 3

$10.00 - $17.99

3-STRING CIGAR BOX GUITAR HYMNALS Volumes 1 & 2

$ 17.99 EA.

CELTIC SONGBOOKS

Irish Drinking Songs, Scottish Favorites, St. Patrick's Day, Irish Love Songs, more...

$ 17.99 - $19.99

WORSHIP LEADER'S HYMNAL

The complete single-volume collection of 113 hymns arranged for 3-string cigar box guitars.

$ 29.99

Shop Now at CBGitty.com/Songbooks

How To Build A Basic 3-String Cigar Box Guitar · Copyright 2019 by Hobo Music Works LLC · All Rights Reserved

Printed in Great Britain
by Amazon